Macdonald Introduction to Technology

Wood Technology

Frederick Oughton

Macdonald
Educational

First published 1975
Macdonald Educational
St Giles House
49–50 Poland Street
London W1A 2LG
ISBN 0 356 05107 2

Series Editor Mary Tapissier
Assistant Editor Jim Miles
Production Philip Hughes
Picture Research Mary Walsh
Design and illustration
Allard Design Group Ltd.

Printed and bound by
Interlitho, Milan, Italy.

The publishers wish to thank the following for assistance given in providing photographs:
Bethnal Green Museum
Buck and Ryan Ltd.
Building Research Establishment
Ciba-Geigy (UK) Ltd.
Council of Forest Industries for British Columbia
Colin Craig
Forestry Commission
Jaycee Furniture Ltd.
Lansing Bagnall Ltd.
London College of Furniture
Metropolitan Museum of Art, Rogers Fund
Don Moss
Musée de l'Ecole de Nancy
National Maritime Museum, London
Reed Paper and Board Co
Rentokil Ltd.
Schloss Charlottenburg, photo W. Steinkopf
Staatsbibliothek, Berlin
Stuart King
Timber Research Development Association
United Africa Co
University of Glasgow, Mackintosh Collection
John Vince
Vosper Thornycroft Ltd.

The cover shows an industrial
circular saw at work.

Contents

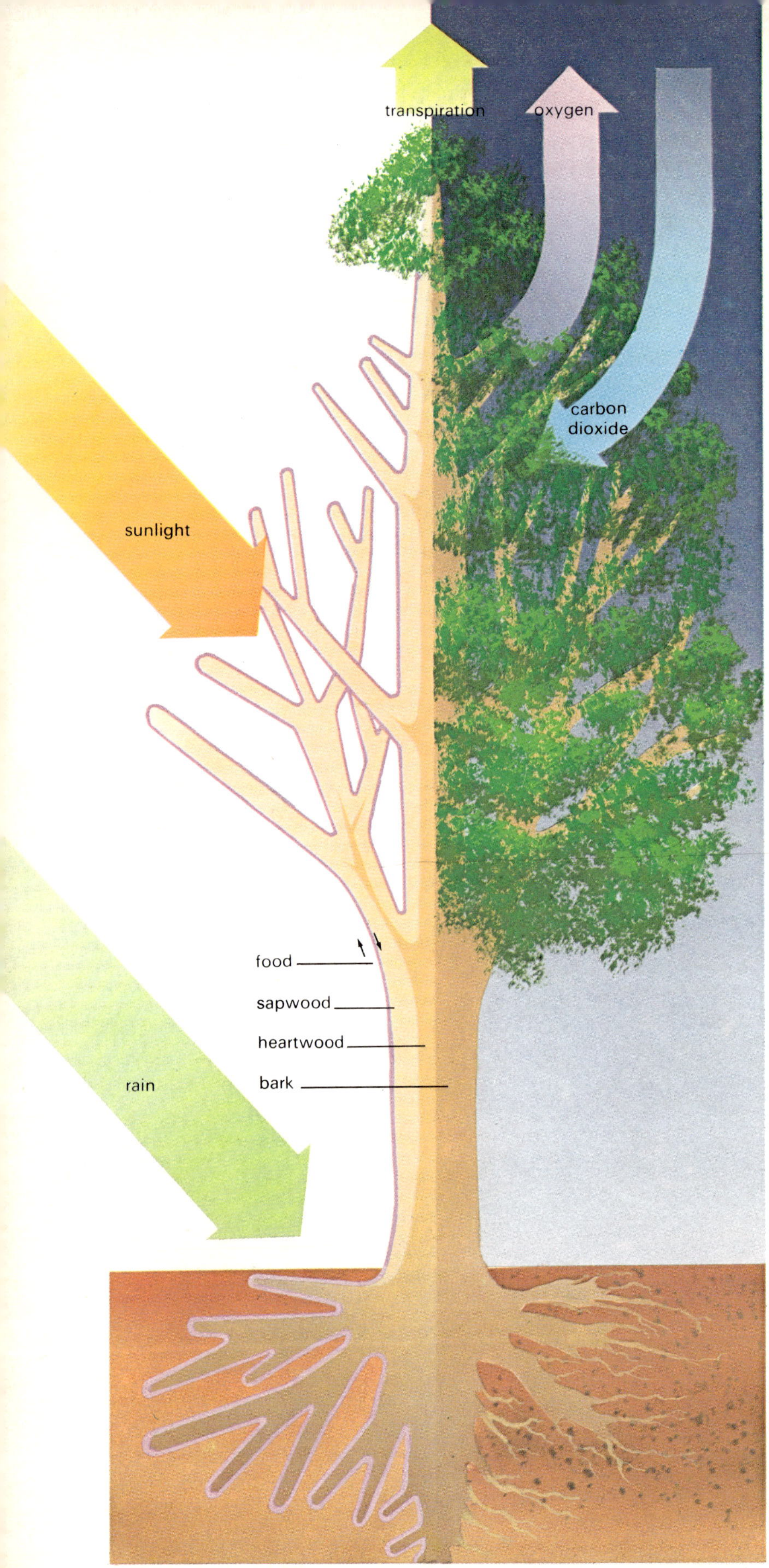

The tree has three parts, each with a specific role to play. They are the roots, stems and leaves.

◀ **Leaves** They take gases from the air, manufacture energy from sunlight and convert the mineral salts which are brought to them from the roots.

◀ **Branches** They carry the intake of the roots to the leaves and act as storage chambers against the time when nourishment is required. They also lift the leaves above any surrounding vegetation and ensure that the tree flourishes. This can be a most important factor in dense forest areas, where much plant life perishes before it can thrive because of overcrowding.

◀ **Roots** They hold the tree firmly in the soil throughout its life, helping to stabilize it by spreading out in a radial pattern. In the fully grown tree they are often equal in length to the height of the topmost branches. Their function is to draw water out of the soil, also to take in essential mineral salts and oxygen for transmission to the rest of the growth.

Growth

In commercial use only the main trunk of a tree has real value. The trunk is enclosed by the bark, which consists of a tough covering to protect the inside of the trunk against the weather, insects and fungi. It is also a conductor, carrying the products of the leaves to the main growth.

Cambium

This is the very thin skin-like tissue which grows between the bark and the wood of the trunk and stems. It is part of the "anatomy and physiology" of the tree, growing both inwards and outwards to form wood and bark respectively. The reason for the trunk of the tree becoming wider in girth is due to the growth of the cambial sheath. During the part of the season when it is not actively growing, it becomes tough and unyielding. While actively growing, it is moist and easily damaged, but it is protected by the bark.

Pith and growth rings

Pith is located at the centre of the stem, and in many trees is very small in circumference. It is surrounded by heart-wood, spring-wood and summer-wood, all of which form concentric circles. Each layer is produced by the cambium during the growing season. In some trees it is possible to distinguish between early and late wood, the early wood being more porous and softer than the late wood.

Cells

Timber is composed of cells. They are brick or tube shaped, some are empty while others contain solid or fluid substances. The tree grows because the number of the cells increases. In the trunk of the tree cell growth is in the cambial tissue. This causes a thickening which goes on more or less evenly throughout the life of the tree.

Sapwood and heartwood

Heartwood is generally darker than sapwood. In many timber-producing areas large quantities of sapwood are wasted, because it is wet and commonly regarded as inferior for commercial purposes.

When both sapwood and heartwood have much the same moisture content, they have an equivalent strength. One major drawback to sapwood is that it tends to attract certain insects and it is open to attack by fungi. When used for construction purposes in damp climates, it rapidly deteriorates and rots unless precautions are taken against this.

Figuring

Straight The fibres run parallel to the vertical axis of the tree. When the trunk is sawn, there are no visual features. The advantage is both economical and functional, because there is little wastage, and straight-grained timber is used extensively for construction work.

Irregular This is generally caused by cutting through a trunk in which there are knots, which cause patterns to appear in the sawn surface.

Diagonal Often caused by incorrect sawing. Timber with a diagonal figuring is unreliable because the angle of cut makes it weak.

Spiral Certain trees will occasionally develop a corkscrew spiral, either along the whole or part of the trunk, running to right or left. Spiral figuring may look highly decorative, but it should not be used for load bearing.

Interlocked Has a striped appearance which is a valuable asset in veneer manufacture and panelling.

Wavy When sawn, the figuring has a rippled appearance. It is much sought after in the furniture industry.

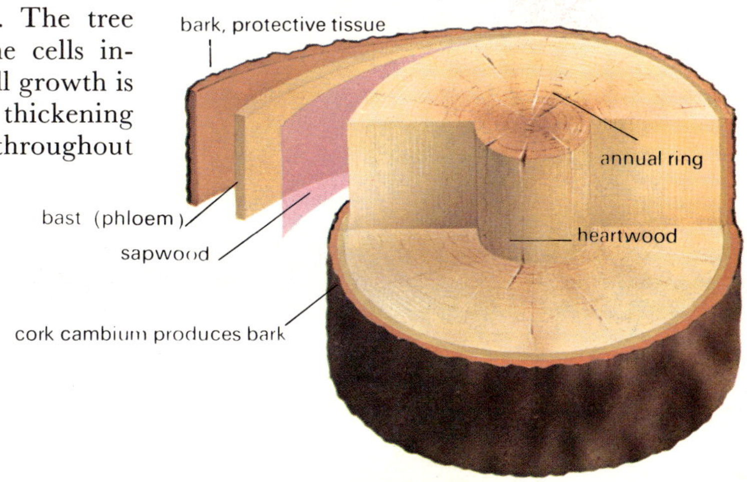

► A layer of sapwood and heartwood is produced by the cambium each year. Together, the sapwood and heartwood make one annual ring. In autumn and winter the tree rests.

Forestry management

Centuries ago, when great swathes of many continents were practically covered and even overgrown with virgin forest, people simply took an axe and chopped down whatever they happened to need in order to build a house, make furniture and use as kindling, and that was the end of the matter. In some areas they cleared the ground either to grow food or else moved on and left areas to naturally regenerate themselves. In other parts they unwittingly destroyed slow-growing trees, creating a scarcity of certain types of timber. In the 13th century entire forests of oak in Germany vanished within a few years, just as many exotic timbers are now being cleared from the Matto Grosso in Brazil to make way for the building of cities and roads. By the start of the 19th century in the United States there was a widening appreciation of the importance of conservation and the need to re-stock areas after trees had been felled. Gifted amateur ecologists explored the possibilities of conserving certain areas, recommendations were drafted and approved by the US government.

In Sweden, which has always been timber-intensive, the growing of trees has been regarded as an industry for more than a century. In Britain with its lack of conservationists, many

▲ This aerial view of a commercially cultivated forest shows the separated areas of the different species of trees.

Economical felling consists of the best possible use being made of people, machines and transportation. Depending on the girth of trees to be felled, the work cycle is first decided and timing agreed upon, and the foresters then divide into teams. One makes the preliminary cuts in the selected trees, followed up by the chainsaw operators, who cut through the main trunk section, while the third team supervise the actual dropping of the tree in a preselected area. After this the trunk is stripped of superficial growth, and prepared for transportation. Successful forest management consists not only of the growing of good timber but also keeping a constant watch over the area. Fire is the chief hazard, especially in conifer belts, hence the system of firebreaks, which in many cases also serve as access roads for the transportation of timber and machinery. Forest supervisors work in close collaboration with wildlife and plant conservationists to maintain the balance of nature which is vital to the wellbeing of the forest.

areas were stripped of oak so that nowadays what used to be an island with huge groves of ancient free-growing oaks is a country in which the remaining specimens are now zealously protected. In practically every country people began too late to regard the tree as something more than a producer of raw material and saw it as a part of the essential ecology. They were ultimately forced to bring into play new methods such as planned planting in their efforts to save and replace what they had destroyed. Already many areas had been completely stripped of wood, if not for conventional structural purposes then, in some countries, for shipbuilding or even for fuel.

Aims

As in other sciences, forestry has its own ideal goal, namely the growing by the fastest possible means a breed of tree, the timber of which has no flaws. The goal has not yet been attained, but work continues. It involves the use of the laboratory in which specialist researchers examine the chromosome structure of many different species. This is backed by work in the seed orchards in which young trees, or saplings, are grown. The seed-bearing branches of the best of the older stock from the larger plantations are grafted on to the sapling. This brings together the superior qualities of both youth and age, and from this union is bred a stronger and sturdier tree in which the predominant features are all good rather than a mixture of good and bad. In the nursery pollination is controlled to the same fine degree that a stud of thoroughbred horses is controlled. In due course the best of the "blueblood" trees are planted in the larger forest areas. In the major forests of the world seed is often "packaged" in soil pellets and then sown from low-flying aircraft.

Felling

Side by side with this programme of maturing trees, the felling continues. Not all are felled, however. The best are left with ample space around them to provide stock for nursery grafting. Felled trees are usually rough-trimmed on the spot and made ready for transportation, but in countries like Canada and the United States the trees are cut into chips, bagged and then taken to a central point for shipment to the paper mills.

▶ Depending on the girth of the tree, hand felling is done with axes and steel wedges, which are hammered into the axe-cut slot to make the tree fall in a definite direction. Trees over 2·5m (8ft) in girth are felled by chain sawing. The chain saw is a diesel or petrol-fuelled continuous-blade tool which can be operated by one person. If the fellers are using one of the larger saws, they wear a harness to stabilize it.

World distribution

Map of the world showing the distribution of hardwood and softwood suitable for commercial use.

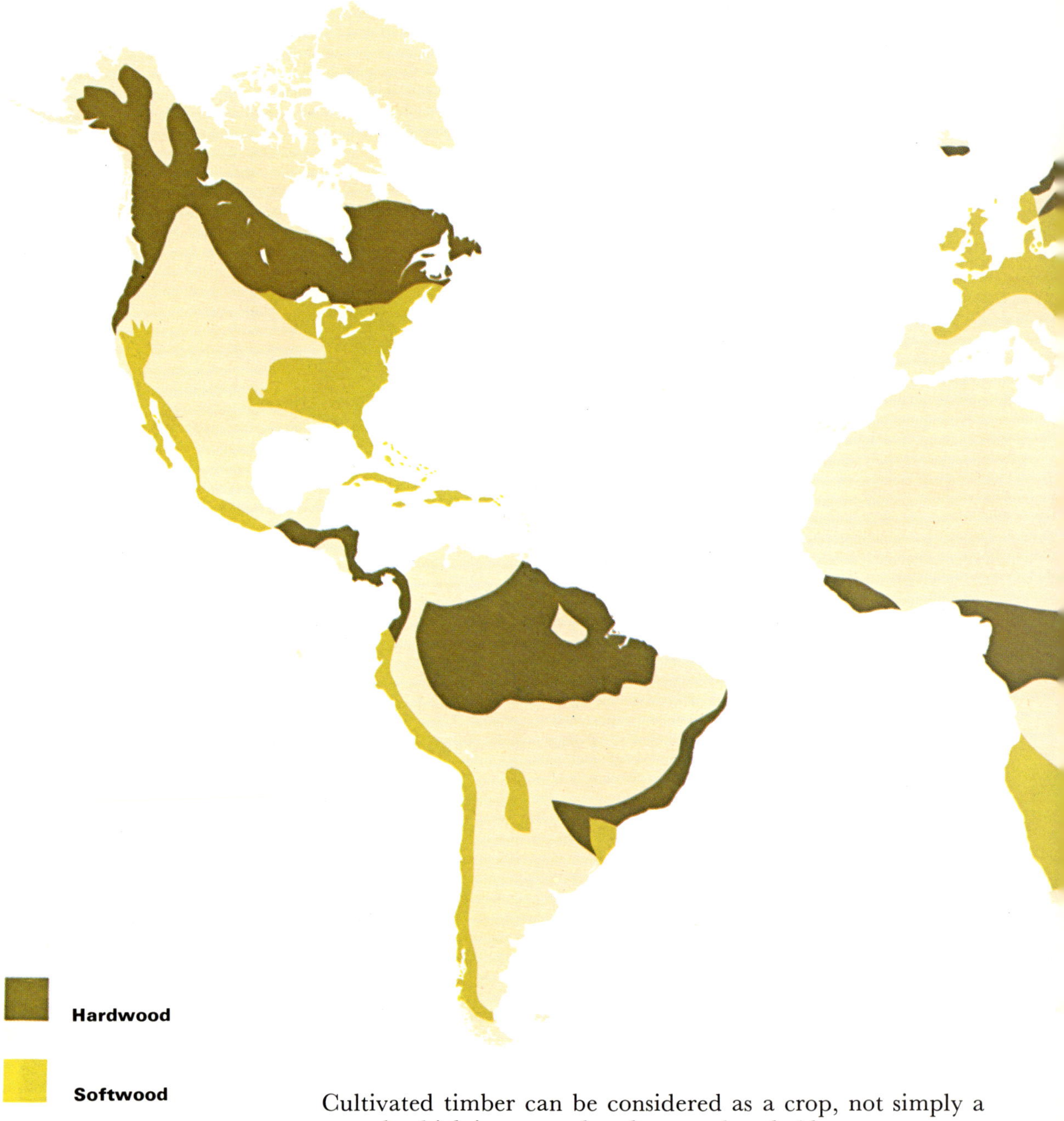

Cultivated timber can be considered as a crop, not simply a growth which is removed and not replaced. About 25 per cent of the land area of the world is covered with forest, amounting to 4000 million hectares (8000 million acres). Only 1500 million hectares (3000 million acres) are being used commercially. The rest is virtually untouched due to labour and transportation problems. Between 1950 and 1968 the most productive commercial areas were Asia, North America and Africa.

Hardwoods merge gradually with the line of softwoods throughout the world regions. Pine, spruce, oak, ash and maple will grow together, but the hardwoods take over on the southern areas of the conifer's natural habitat. Oak, ash, elm, beech, sweet chestnut, walnut and sycamore, alder, willow, lime, cherry and poplar are found growing together throughout Europe and in the Eastern United States and Southern Ontario.

Hardwoods fall into three categories, those which are soft and light, others which are medium hard and heavy, and those which are extremely hard and heavy.

Softwoods grow in a belt which covers the northern areas of the globe, including Scotland, Scandinavia, the Baltic regions, Russia and Siberia, also Eastern Canada to the Rockies and the Pacific Coast from Alaska to California. The southern edge leads to a mixed growth of softwood and hardwood into the north temperate zone, and it includes Britain, France, Germany and Central Europe. Softwoods also grow in subtropical zones, and conifers have now found a foothold in Mexico. This illustrates the adaptability of some species.

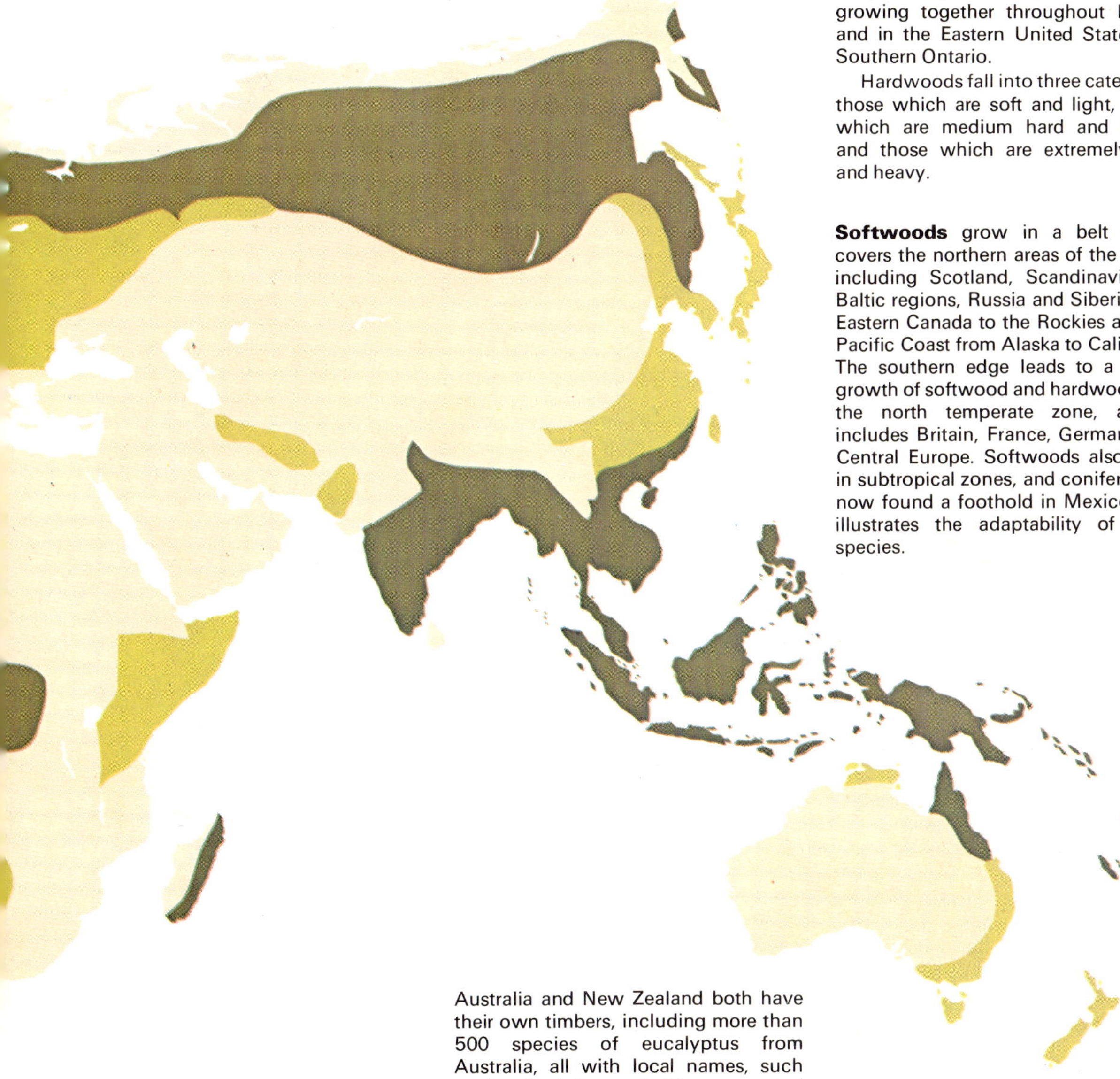

Australia and New Zealand both have their own timbers, including more than 500 species of eucalyptus from Australia, all with local names, such as jarrah, tallowood, blue gum and Karri.

There are more than 40,000 types of trees, but only 10,000 have any economic status. In most countries there are alien species which have been imported over a period of years for growing purposes. Some have succeeded, some have failed. For present purposes we are looking only at commercially grown timber. Starting at the areas in which there are commercially-operated forests, we have: *softwoods*—conifers; *softwoods and hardwoods*—mixed crops; *hardwoods*—tropical; *hardwoods*—temperate.

Identification

oak

ash

spruce

beech

mahogany (Honduras)

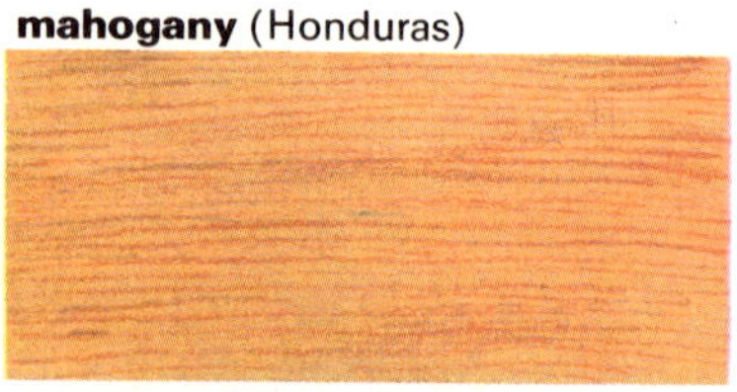

mahogany (Africa)

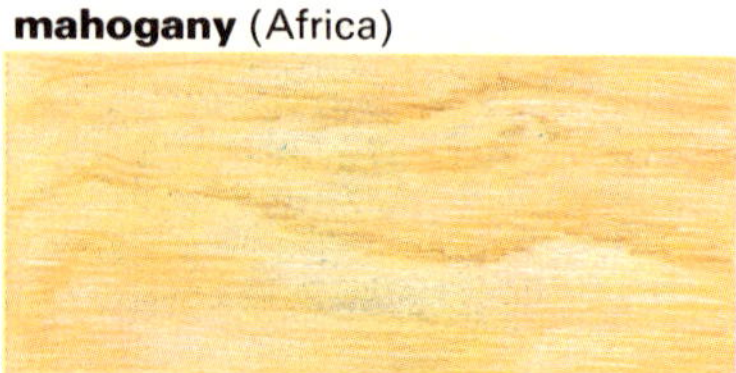

teak

There are more than 20,000 species of timber, but no truly efficient international system of identification has yet been devised to cover them all. Different countries use totally different names for the same timber or for timbers of a similar nature. In some cases a colloquial name for a particular species may be universally recognized. Because comparatively few species are commercially cultivated, despite a world shortage of timber of all kinds, the ordinary timber merchant is seldom familiar with more than a few types. Shortage has led to intensive research into ways and means of improving timber utilization.

Moisture

Water influences the way timber reacts. Its presence gives an indication of long-term shrinkage and resistance to insects and decay. The amount of moisture is worked out by using this calculation:

$$\frac{\text{Weight of water present}}{\text{Dry weight of wood substance}} \times 100$$

In order to determine the moisture content, the oven-dry method is used. This consists of:

$$\frac{\text{Initial weight of sample} - \text{dry weight of sample}}{\text{Dry weight of sample}} \times 100$$

"Initial weight" means weight when the test is done. "Dry weight" means weight after moisture has been dried out.

The apparatus used is an accurate balance and a constant-temperature electrical oven capable of operating at between 95°C and 105°C (205°–220°F) with a ventilation system through which steam is drawn.

A sample block, or several blocks of equal size, from the batch of timber, are weighed. This is done without delay, because most timbers immediately begin to draw up moisture from the atmosphere when they are sawn. They are put in the oven at a temperature of 60°C for several hours to slowly draw out moisture. A higher temperature will seal moisture in, making a true estimate of moisture content impossible. The temperature is then raised to 102°C for eight hours, after which the samples are immediately weighed again. Failure to show a lower weight than in the first weighing means that they will be returned to the oven. The process continues until a difference can be noted.

Determination of moisture content helps decide whether a particular batch of timber can be used for external or internal, specific or general purposes. The method can also be applied while timber is seasoning, samples being taken from different parts of the kiln.

Oils and resins

These substances can cause a substantial margin of error when moisture is being calculated. It applies only to certain timbers, such as pitch pine. To allow for oils and resins, 50g (2oz) of sawdust are placed in a flask with low-density water-soluble oil. The apparatus consists of a water bath in which the flask is placed. To the flask is attached a condenser, graduated receiver and draw-off cock. Oils and resins are drawn off, and the percentage of moisture content is estimated by applying the following:

$$\frac{\text{Weight in grams of water collected}}{\text{Initial weight of weighed sample} - \text{weight in grams of water collected}} \times 100$$

Moisture meters

There are alternative methods of determining moisture content. They are electrical appliances which operate on the principle that the electrical resistance of timber can represent a moisture-content index, degree of measurement being from 6 to 24 per cent. Although many varieties of meter are in use, all are based on one of two systems. The first uses the electrical capacitance of timber, the second measures the electrical resistance. In the capacitance method sharp probe-type electrodes are pushed deeply into the timber, and the moisture content is read from a scale. In the electrical-resistance method two contact plates are used with a variable condenser, one on either side of the timber sample and the moisture content registers on a scale.

Fibre saturation point

The term describes the situation in which the water in the timber lies between the cells and is removed, leaving the cell walls themselves still saturated. The walls can contain between 25 and 30 per cent of their dry weight in water before they equal the saturation point of the connective fibres. When cell walls lose water, timber shrinks. Some timbers can absorb or discharge more than others, but all have a limit. This is inherent in the nature of the timber itself, and it is a factor which cannot be modified by seasoning.

Differential shrinkage

This is the movement which occurs during seasoning. Certain types of mahogany have very little shrinkage, which makes them suitable for any work in which maximum stability is needed. In general, shrinkage is more pronounced in hardwoods than in softwoods.

Factors like shrinkage and the other behavioural characteristics of individual timbers have their own importance. These factors mean it is possible to evaluate the performance of individual timbers in any given environment. One example is the recent introduction of central heating in a house panelled in the 17th century. When the temperature rose only a few degrees, the ancient timber, which had been completely stable for 300 years, began to shrink.

Moisture contained in an oak furniture section

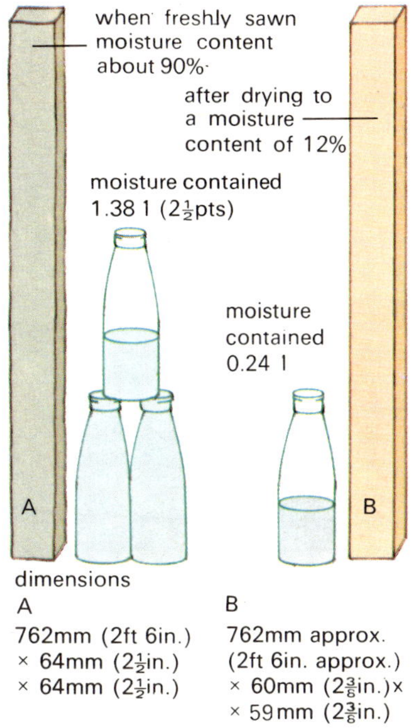

▲ The amount of moisture which can be drawn off any section of timber without affecting the working properties is governed to some extent by the nature of the wood itself, but also by the quantity which can be safely removed. Softwood reacts more violently than hardwood, but if seasoning is skilfully regulated, the properties of softwood are preserved.

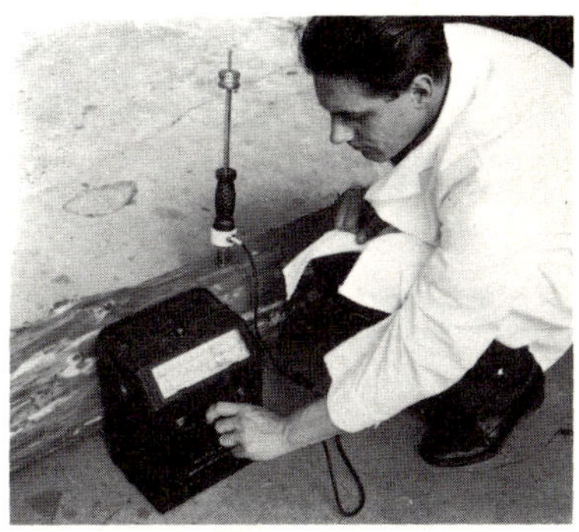

▲ Moisture meter in use to check the moisture content of wood either before or after air or kiln seasoning. This tool reads off the moisture, which is between 6 and 24 per cent. The tool can be used by an untrained operative, because it is necessary only to attach it to the sample timber and then read off the amount of moisture on a calibrated dial.

▲ A typical timber structure in which stressing and loading creates an overall stability and rigidity. Most American frame houses of the 18th and 19th centuries were built to this pattern.

▲ The behaviour of timber under stress is observed in the laboratory. Laminated timbers of different species and in a variety of forms are used, such as arches and roof trusses.

The following are the main categories in which individual timbers are classified as far as their vital physical properties are concerned. **Forces/loads** refer to the amount of external loading required before a specimen piece of timber alters its shape. These shape changes are caused because the external loading creates internal forces. They are called **stresses**. In the timber testing laboratory a stress is expressed as gramms per square centimetre or lbs/sq.ft. Shape change is noted and carefully measured. It is called **deformation**. Certain timbers will revert to their original shape after stress testing, depending on their overall composition and characteristics. This ability is regulated in all types of timber by the quality of **elasticity**. It is possible to forecast fairly accurately the elasticity of a piece of any given dimensions on the basis of a small sample. Part of this forecast is called **the limit of proportionality**. Once the limit of what the timber will bear under loading is reached, it is known that deformation will increase far more rapidly than the rate of loading. The point at which the deformation will become permanent is **permanent set**. This may also be termed the limit of elasticity of the timber beyond which the piece finally breaks. When this point is reached, it is called **maximum load**. This means the point at which the fibres of the timber actually separate.

Physical properties

Certain timbers are used for certain jobs, not because they seem to be right but because they possess special qualities unique to themselves.

Interplay of forces

Depending on the use of the timber, one or more forces may be at play. Laboratories use such expressions as "comprehensive stress", meaning a combination of several forces, "stiffness" when the timber will not bend in a manner which is in character with its usual nature, and "modulus of elasticity". This is the relation between strain and stress, taking into account the "limit of proportionality".

Toughness

This can be summed up in several ways, and it does not refer only to the ability of the wood to resist a series of blows, but to the point at which it will split and break. There is also shock resistance, measured as a rule by dropping a weight from a fixed height. There is also the total work which can be done during bending—for instance, the behaviour of the timber when it is bent and nails or spikes are driven into it.

Timber as a fuel

East and West Africa and South-East Asia all make extensive use of wood fuels. In Tanzania, for instance, wood-fuel consumption amounts to 96 per cent of total timber consumption. Industries in these countries also consume large quantities of timber fuel for tobacco curing, the making of cassava meal, tin smelting and sugar production.

A recent survey by the Food and Agriculture Organization of the United Nations showed that between them Tanzania, Gambia and Thailand used over 85 per cent, or about 2000 million tonnes (tons) (air dry) of total wood consumption per year. Other research showed that the world as a whole burns 2300 million tonnes (tons) of wood annually. This is equal to the use of 1300 million tonnes (tons) of coal. Africa and South America represent 50 per cent of the total forest area of the world. It is now planned to create special forest areas devoted only to the growing of fuelwoods, such as eucalyptus and other quick growing species with a yield of approximately 4 tonnes per hectare (8 tons per acre) per year, which represents an average family consumption.

One by-product of these fuelwood plantations could be material made from wood fibre and used in low-sulphur petroleum production. Pilot experiments suggest that one tonne (ton) of woodfuel can produce two barrels of oil. At a time when large areas of the world are suffering from economic crisis due to the increase in the price of oil by relatively few oil-producing nations, this and other fuel-producing possibilities have gained priority in research and development programmes.

Seasoning

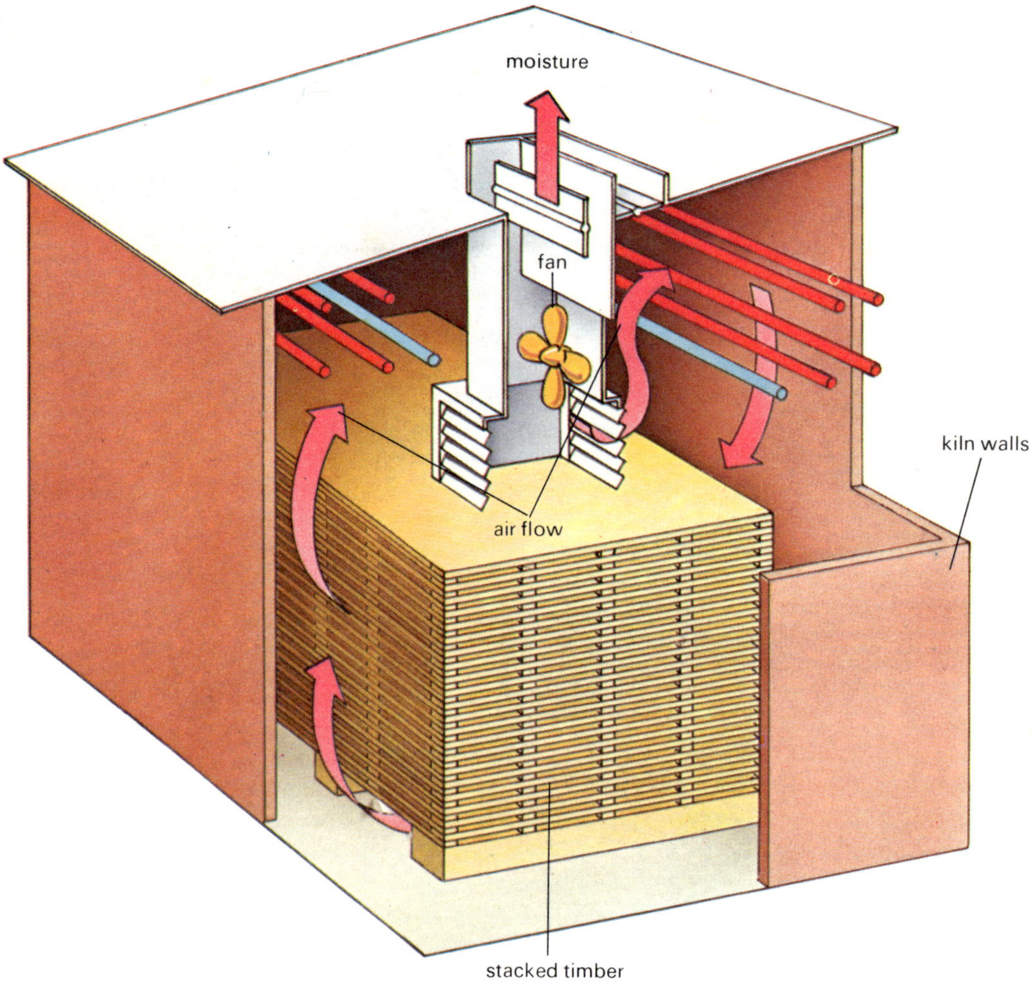

Timber has to be stabilized in its external and internal structure before it can be used for furniture making and building. This is called seasoning. The process also prevents infestation by some insects and fungi, which can weaken and stain timber. It lessens weight by reduction of moisture content, leading to substantial shipping economies. Certain timbers are stored for 20 or more years. The longer timber is seasoned and properly stored, the better the quality.

During seasoning one danger is that drying begins from the outside and finishes while the interior is still wet, which causes splits, ruptures and fractures. Successful seasoning balances evaporation between exterior and interior. Three factors, humidity, circulation and air temperature, are vital.

▲ The heated kiln is airtight and has steam sprays. Advanced kilns have fans to accelerate air flow. Heat comes from steam-heated coils over which air passes before it moves over and through the timber stacks. A certain amount of controlled humidity is used.

▶ During seasoning and storage timber must be stacked in such a way that air can freely circulate around it. Thin slivers of the same type of timber are used to interleave the layers, the number of slivers being determined by the lengths, taking into account any tendency to bow or warp. In modern timber-processing plants handling is done mechanically, and the stackings are laid on pallets.

▼ Timber stacked in an open-sided drying shed. The timber is arranged to allow the maximum natural circulation of air.

Air seasoning

This is done by laying up the logs in sheds, protected from the weather but still permitting prevailing winds to circulate around them. A more elaborate shed is a brick building with louvred walls or panels, which can be open and shut to guide air flow. This method of seasoning is used for valuable exotic woods, but not generally for common softwoods.

Timber is not stacked surface against surface. It is separated by stickers, which are strips of softwood, used to avoid making indentations which cause expensive wastage. Stickers are carefully selected for each job. Their thickness is economically important. If 2cm (1in) boards are piled with 2cm (1in) stickers at 0·5m (2ft) intervals, this gives a sticker volume of about 4 per cent of the stack. The thicker the stickers, the faster the seasoning.

Kiln seasoning

This is done in a closed compartment in which air circulation can be controlled and timber drying regulated. Kilning means that a much lower moisture content of the timber is reached.

This method has three main advantages: precision, adaptability of the kiln and speed. A kiln can be used all the year round and give predictable results in contrast to air seasoning, which depends on the weather. Kilning also destroys fungus and insects, and any resin or gum in the timber is baked hard. Softwoods stand up well to kilning, but hardwoods have to be treated with care. Many kilns are heated by burning the waste products of the sawmill.

The heated kiln is airtight and has steam sprays. Advanced kilns have fans to accelerate air flow. Heat comes from steam-heated coils over which air passes before it moves over and through the timber stacks. A certain amount of controlled humidity is used, and in forced-circulation kilns the air is changed at intervals.

Defects

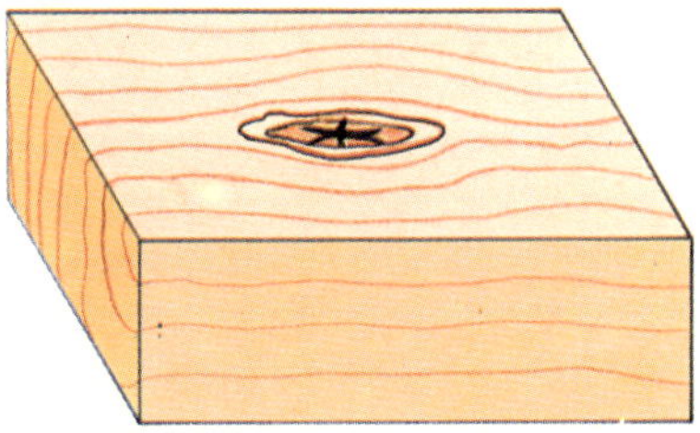

Knots form during increase of diameter of the tree, when branches sprout from the trunk. The point at which branch and trunk meet forms a knot. Knots can seriously weaken the strength of timber, especially in construction work.

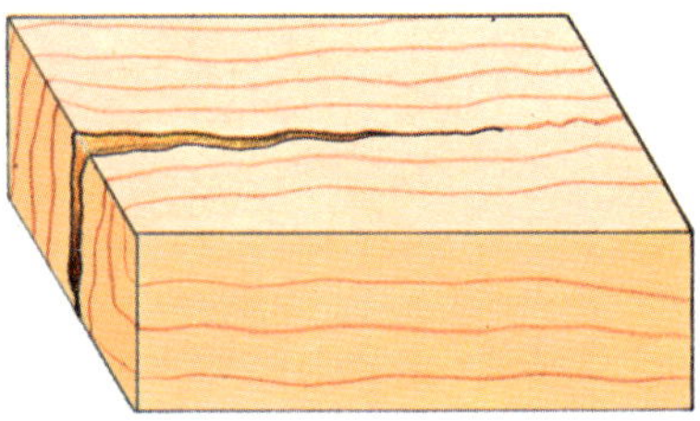

Shakes are splits caused by opening of the grain. They occur mostly in softwoods, but also in one hardwood family.

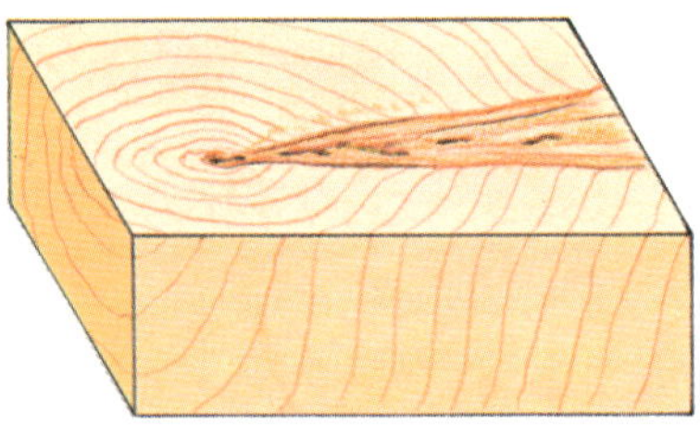

Bark pockets are caused by damage to the cambium, or thin tissue forming a sheath between trunk, or bole, and branches. Bark is occluded, or drawn, into the main body, and may cause rotting of growth in the immediate vicinity.

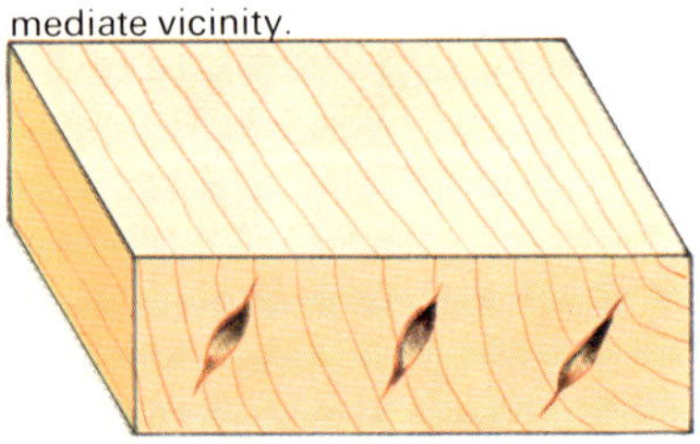

Latex canals can produce shakes when timber is seasoned. They are tubular or cellular caused by latex storage during tree growth.

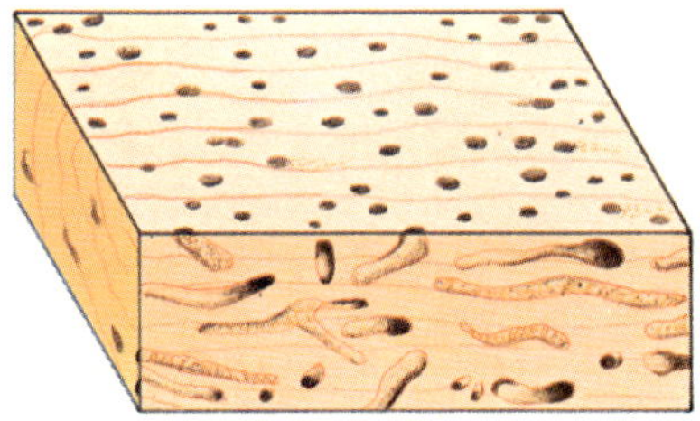

Death-watch beetle lays eggs in cracks and crevices of ancient timber. To survive it needs a certain amount of moisture. The tunnels and galleries are extensive and are left full of impacted dust.

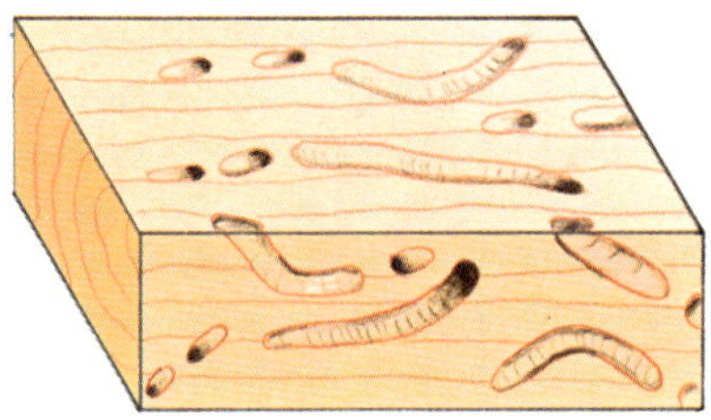

Powder-post beetle larvae live on the starch content of wood, and eat the walls of the starch cells. Of the several species all can do substantial damage to timber.

Compression failure consists of haphazard hairline cracks running across the grain in the middle of the main trunk. It shows up during seasoning, developing rapidly into a series of splits. Failure occurs at a later stage, when the piece breaks into several pieces during handling.

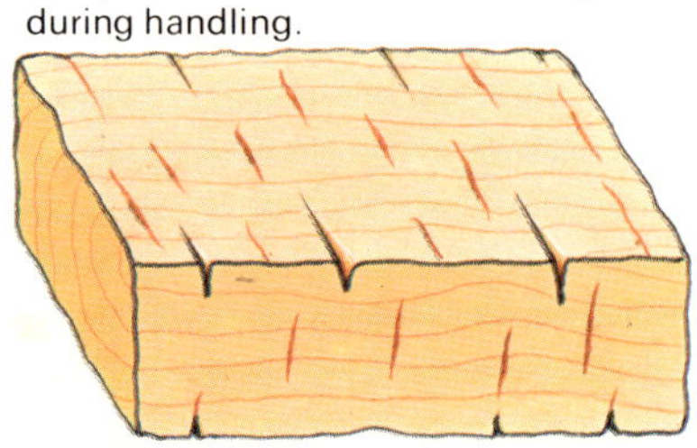

Gum veins are typified by dark streaks running like canals along the grain. In some timbers, such as African walnut, they may have a decorative appearance.

Pith flecks are due to tunnelling by insect larvae. Tunnels may be narrow but still sufficient to cause discolouration after the piece is sawn.

Strawberry marks are generally found in Sitka spruce in the form of circular red areas, but sometimes as a straight broad bar running across the sawn piece. They are caused by accumulation of resin.

Lack of proper control in seasoning causes faults like "cupping", which is a curving of the piece; "twisting" or cork-screwing of the timber in one direction or the other; "bowing", which is a sagging in the middle of the piece; "spring", which is longitudinal distortion.

◀ **Mineral streaks** are resin canals which may be light or dark, depending on the natural hue of the timber. They do not seriously interfere with the strength of the material.

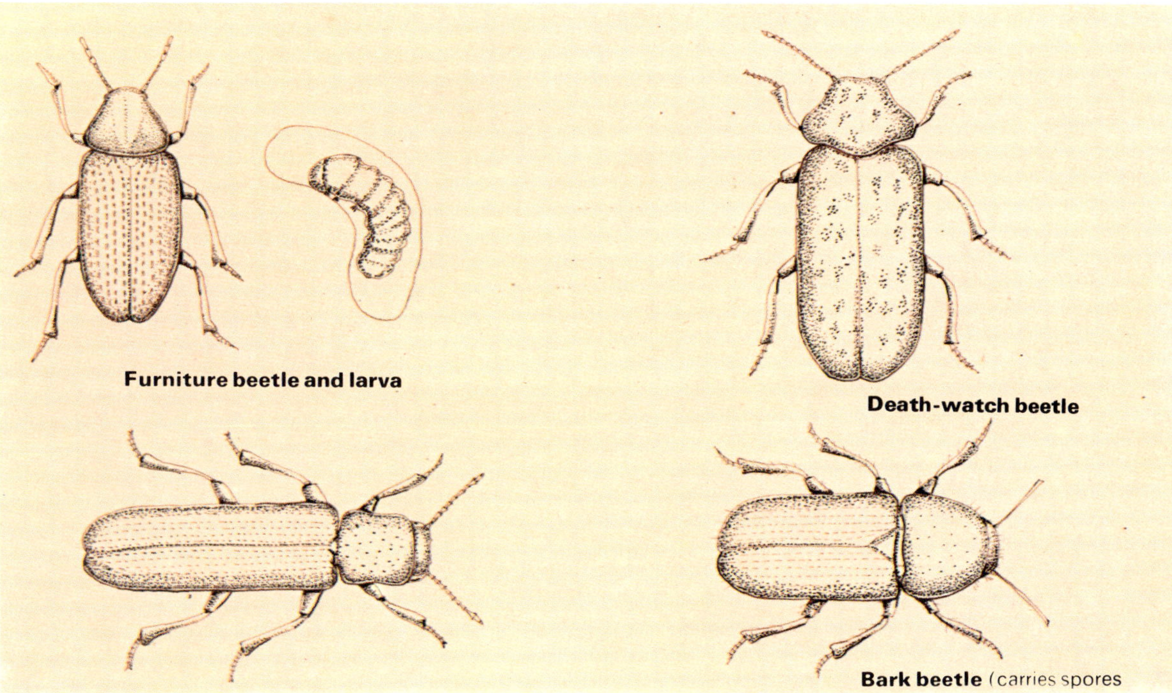

Furniture beetle and larva

Death-watch beetle

Powder-post beetle

Bark beetle (carries spores of the fungus which cause "Dutch Elm" disease)

Few timbers are free from natural defects. In some timbers the defects can be used to advantage in veneers, interior decoration and the making of fine furniture.

Insects

"Woodworm" is a term in general use to cover many different wood-boring and wood-eating insects, some of which can attack wood when it is submerged for long periods in the sea, and others in the forest, the seasoning shed or timber yard. Each of them inhabits different environments, and most of them cannot withstand transition from one environment to another.

Longhorn beetles lay eggs under the bark of newly-cut trees, and larvae feed on the wood, making holes up to 2·5cm (1in) in diameter. Holes are full of "frass" or dust. Larvae can be destroyed by heat sterilization. They are common in northern Europe.

Pinhole borer larvae eat the mould fungus conveyed by the adult borers. This fungus grows on the gallery walls and is known as "ambrosia" fungus. The beetles tunnel into living trees, building special egg chambers. Empty chambers become filled with resin and other organic materials.

Common furniture beetle lives in dead trees and in seasoned hard and softwood. Larvae hatch from eggs in minute cracks, working their way along the grain and forming long tunnels, which weaken the structure.

Termites are found in the tropics and subtropics, and can be divided into subterranean and dry-wood varieties. They attack timber in patches, leaving large pockets of hollowed-out wood with an outside shell which eventually collapses. Dry-wood termites burrow into areas just below the surface and work rapidly, leaving a honeycomb of rotten timber.

Preservation

No timber can be preserved indefinitely, but in some circumstances it can have a life of several hundred years, depending on the atmospheric conditions. Timber is destroyed by insects, mechanical faults or fire.

Timber has a low thermal conductivity, and can be treated to make it either fire-retarding or fire-proof. Salts used for these treatments were introduced in 1821, but the modern method is to use fire-retarding paint containing sodium silicate, water and kaolin. Because the specific heat of timber is high and conductivity is low, all-timber buildings have less fire risk than those built of other materials.

Preservatives include tar-oil made from creosote, and water-soluble salts, which include salts of copper, potassium and arsenic. Organic preservatives are toxic and soluble in petroleum oils, but have the advantage of being permanent for interior and exterior use. Application is by dipping, spraying or brushing.

Hand tools

◀ A medieval woodcut showing woodworking craftsmen using adze-type tools and saws. Tools were often primitive but effective, and trestles rather than benches were used for the sake of portability and flexibility. In some cases beams for roofing support were shaped on the ground, using the long-handled adze, which is still used by African boat builders. Most tools were iron of high quality, because no steel forging was done at that time. Spikes, not nails, were used to hold timber lengths together and jointing was, by modern standards, crude. Tools such as planes were of advanced design in contrast to other implements. Holes were made in wood with augers, fore-runners of the modern auger bit, but at that time fitted with a long shank and a two-sided handle into which extensions could be fitted by the craftsman to provide extra force when boring holes through oak beams which might be over a metre thick. Sawing of timber was done very roughly, using two-handled tools with one sawyer on either end when lengths had to be cut evenly. In most cases the saw had fewer teeth than the modern counterparts, and it must have required great muscular power and people working in relays to successfully cut a piece of oak, which was the most common building material of the time.

A woodworking tool can be anything from a paring knife to a large workshop built for the purpose and containing a dozen planes, hammers of all kinds and weights, saws both long and short, chisels by the dozen.

Chisels

They are as old as woodworking itself, consisting of a wooden handle into which the tang, or metal spike, fits, the metal shank itself and the cutting end, bevelled and kept to a razor-like sharpness by frequent rubbing on an oilstone. Bronze-Age examples show few radical differences between designs then and now, but some of the ancient specimens suggest a careful attention to workmanship and design, because they were drilled with holes to accommodate rivets for fixing the metal section to the wooden handle. In the Iron-Age a flange, or lip, was introduced at the point where the metal part met the handle, and this was done to create greater stability between the sections.

Saws

The idea of mounting the saw in a wooden frame and then tensioning it originated with the Romans. The saw itself was simply a thin strip of toothed metal, enabling the craftsman to execute delicate work.

Saws are available in many varieties. They include the hand saw with between $4\frac{1}{2}$ and 12 points, or teeth, every 25mm (1in) and the tenon with between 14 and 18 teeth every 25mm (1in). The compass-saw cuts curves, while the coping saw does the same job but on a smaller scale. Pad saws have a rounded handle and interchangeable blades, while the long-established bow saw can still be bought in sizes from 15cm to 45cm (6 to 18in).

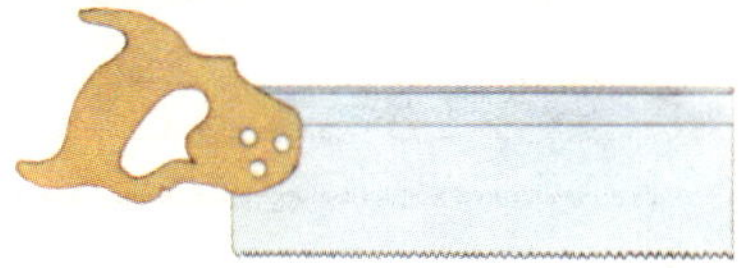

Tenon saw

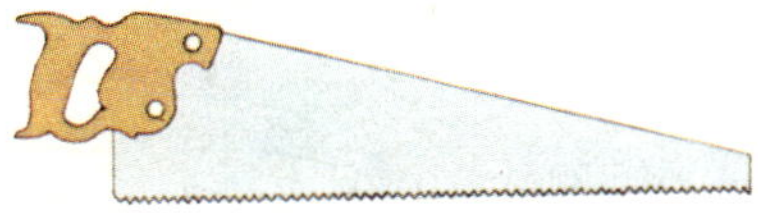

Rip saw

Screwdrivers

The traditional model is the "London" screwdriver in sizes from 7·5cm (3in) to 45cm (18in) with a bulbous handle designed for easy gripping and a brass ferrule to securely hold the blade.

Planes

As with most other hand tools, many planes are made for specific purposes within a certain range, such as the plough plane with its set of 23 interchangeable cutters which, between them, can tackle intricate mouldings for ornamental overmantels and cornices and the decoration of furniture.

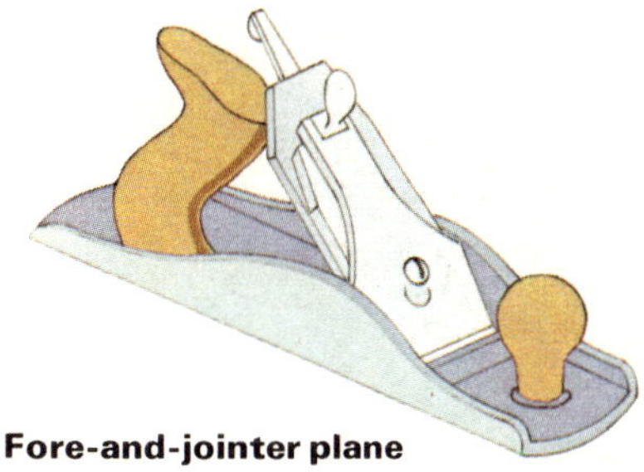

Fore-and-jointer plane

Boring tools

The bow drill, which enabled craftsmen to bore holes faster and more efficiently, made its appearance about 2540 BC and was used continuously until the Middle Ages with few major modifications. It was eventually replaced with the breast auger and the brace drill.

The modern brace and bit was invented in 1864, embodying adjustable jaws in a chuck. The brace is made in a range of sizes, known in the trade as "sweeps", which describes the diameter of the revolution of the brace, being 12, 20, 25, 30 and 35cm (5, 8, 10, 12 and 14in).

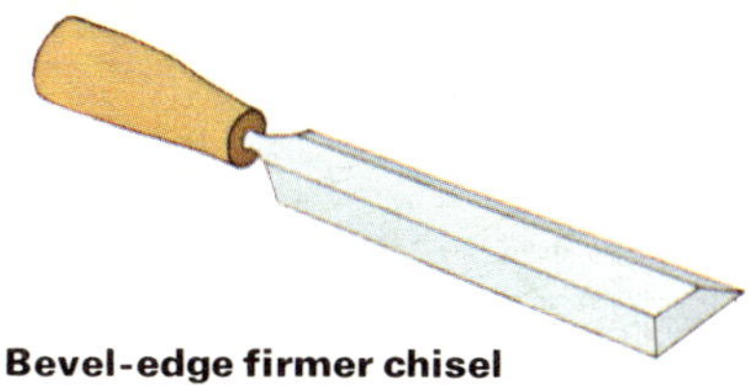

Bevel-edge firmer chisel

Hammers

A well-made hammer has a head secured to the handle with three wedges, two steel and one wood. A pull of more than 4 tonnes (4 tons) is needed to separate head from handle. In the hands of the experienced craftsman a hammer will deliver about 61 joules (45 foot-lbs) with a contact pressure of more than 0·5 tonne ($\frac{1}{2}$ ton) per $25mm^2$ (square inch). Levering a nail out of timber with the adze eye claw of a nailing hammer produces up to 450kg (1000lb) pressure at the point between the handle and the head when the handle is between 30mm and 38mm (12 and 15in) long. Although there are more than 73 different kinds of hammer, many with specific trade applications, most general utility work can be done with a 900g (28oz) adze eye claw, a 450g (16oz) Warrington and, for light work, a 160g ($3\frac{1}{2}$oz) cross pein hammer.

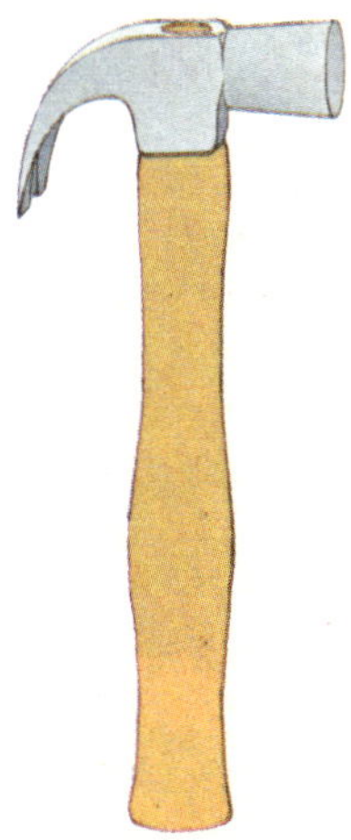

Adze-eye-claw hammer

Power hand tools

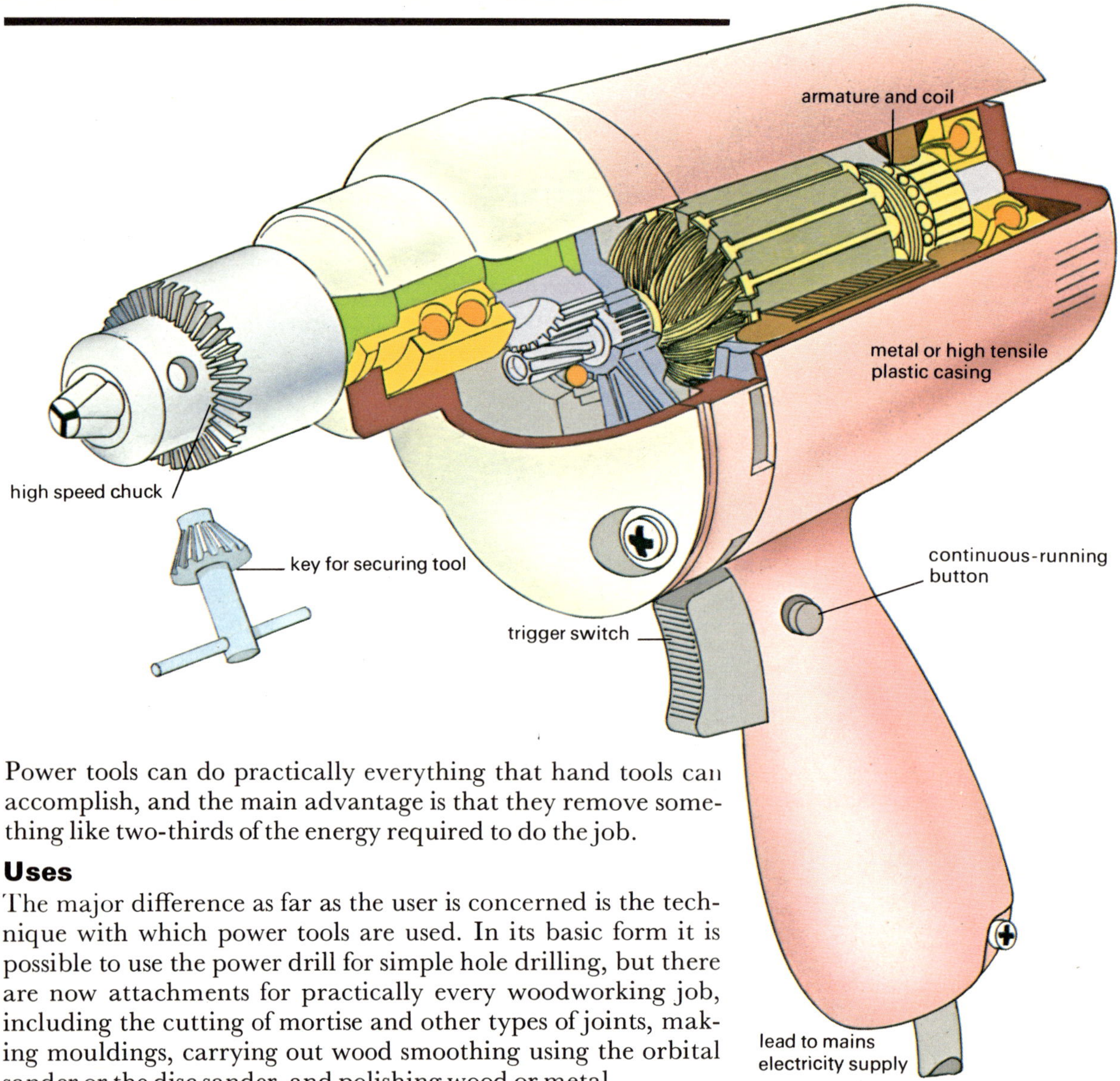

▲ Cutaway view of a typical modern power drill

Power tools can do practically everything that hand tools can accomplish, and the main advantage is that they remove something like two-thirds of the energy required to do the job.

Uses

The major difference as far as the user is concerned is the technique with which power tools are used. In its basic form it is possible to use the power drill for simple hole drilling, but there are now attachments for practically every woodworking job, including the cutting of mortise and other types of joints, making mouldings, carrying out wood smoothing using the orbital sander or the disc sander, and polishing wood or metal.

The power drill can be converted into a wood-turning lathe by attaching it to a lathe bed, when it can be used for making small objects, such as bowls and table and chair legs.

There is another attachment called a *flexible drive*. This consists in effect of a precision-made length of driving section which is connected to the tool-holding chuck. It enables the user to tackle jobs in situations where it is difficult to insert the bulky drill.

The *drill press* is simply an adjustable stand into which the power drill is clamped and can then be lifted and lowered to predetermined measurements, making it possible to mass-produce objects of a high standard.

Power drills are classified by the size of the *chuck*, which is the end-piece used for holding the tool. The usual sizes are 6mm ($\frac{1}{4}$in) and 7mm ($\frac{5}{16}$in).

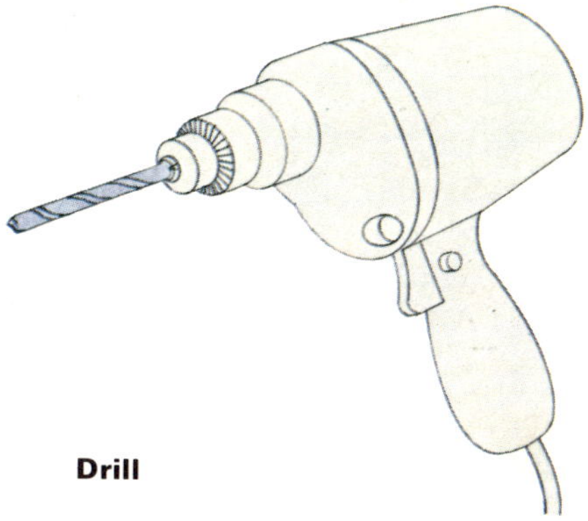

Drill

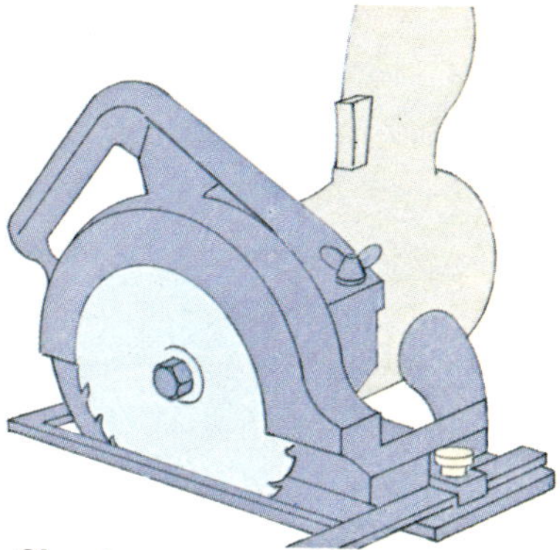

Circular saw

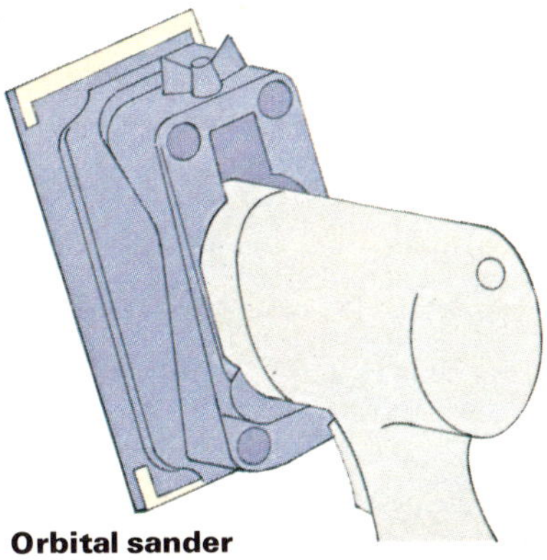

Orbital sander

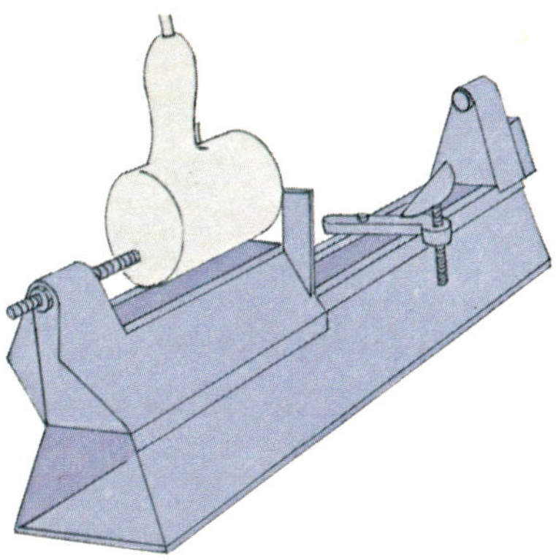

Wood-turning lathe bed

Safety

One of the problems of power hand drills until recently was safety. Many amateurs were electrocuted because they failed to earth the equipment. Drills from different countries were made to various standards, and the user was often at a loss to know how to make the electrical connections in the correct sequence. The problem has now been solved by a system known as double-insulating, using a two-cord cable, which makes it quite safe to attach an electric plug incorrectly. In 1968 the British Factory Inspectorate permitted the use of this system, which has become widespread on industrial premises.

Speed

Operationally, the most important factor in the power drill is the running speed. If it runs too slowly, the tool-head will not function properly, if it runs too quickly, friction can develop and burn the wood. The most common result of many years of research and development is the two- or three-speed electric drill so that most have two speeds, giving a speed of about 20,000 rev./min. in the main shaft of the armature, which is geared down to 3000 rev./min. Many models generate air through a duct located at the front of the tool to blow away wood dust as it accumulates, keeping this area of the workpiece free and easy to see.

Not all power-drill jobs can be done at the same speed, so speed reducers are now being incorporated for use where the generation of heat by friction is undesirable.

Amateurs use power drills for many jobs, including the shaping and contouring of wood. Rotary files are used for this purpose. This makes it possible to cut elaborate mouldings for use on furniture and general decoration.

Drills can also be used as the basis of a saw table. They can not only cut wood, but also with a mitreing attachment can make precision joints. It takes about 50 seconds to saw a 5x10cm (2x4in) piece of timber, but when a power saw is used the time is reduced to only three seconds. A mitre-cut for a joint can be cut by hand in 90 seconds, whereas a power tool will do the same job, with more precision, in ten seconds.

Sabre saw

The sabre saw is an integrated tool, made specially for the job it has to do, but still using much the same kind of electric motor as in the power saw. The saw itself is operated by a cranking action from the driving gear, creating a reciprocal blade action of up to 3300 up-and-down movements per minute. The blade is not very long but it is available in a variety of teeth-per-centimetre (inch) types. The seven-teeth per 2·5cm (1in) type is used for rough shaping the wood, while the ten-tooth is for both hard and softwoods, and the same length and teeth-per-centimetre (inch) saw is used for cutting plywood.

Sabre saws are fitted with a "shoe", similar in shape to the one on a sewing machine, through which the saw passes, stabilizing the cutting section on the surface of the wood. The sabre saw is used in the woodworking industry for cutting the inside curves of contoured kitchen and other furniture.

Engineering systems

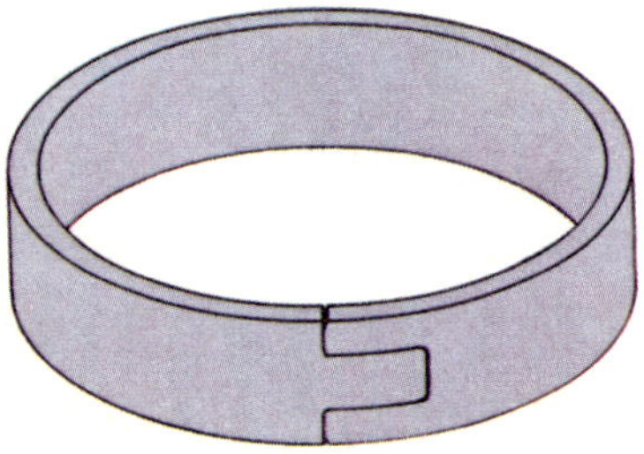

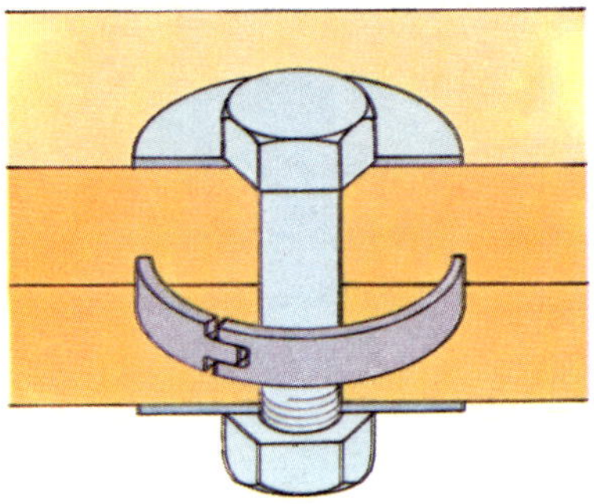

▲ **Split-ring connector** for making a timber-to-timber joint, working on the principle of a tongue and slot and providing for the expansion and contraction of the two pieces of timber.

Wood was used for building purposes as early as 8000 BC, but there was very little systematic knowledge about the characteristics of individual timbers until 1678, when Robert Hooke investigated problems of stress and strain. Then about 250 years passed before science investigated other utilization problems.

Specific strength

Specific strength is a key factor. It means the ratio of strength to any given unit weight. In efficient design timber does not undergo simultaneously such forces as *compression* (the minimum force required to crush or break the wood), *tension* (the amount of force needed to pull the piece in two) and *shear* (the force needed to crack the timber in two). Modern design techniques ensure a fair load distribution. By using the formula: "if two sections are geometrically similar and have much the same weight, a cross section may vary inversely to the density raised to the power of 1·5", it has been found that timber struts have many advantages over steel joists of equivalent or much greater length.

Tests show that timber can be used for roofing, large-span aircraft hangers, some types of warehousing, towers and other tall, thin constructions. Much depends on the uses to which such constructions are put and to the methods of fixing one piece of timber to another. This is done with connectors.

Connectors

The *Kubler dowel*, a piece of hardwood, was an early connector. Its shape was doubly conical, widest in the middle and bored straight through with a hole to take a bolt. The two pieces of timber to be joined in an interface were bored to take the dowel and the bolt with a nut to tighten it and hold it in position.

The *bulldog connector* developed from the Kubler dowel and is still in use. It can be either round or square, and is made of steel with a bolt hole through the middle. The nut is tightened, forcing the teeth of the plate into the wood.

Split-ring connectors are fitted with grooves which have their counterparts precut in both pieces of timber, and drawn together by a bolt in much the same way as the bulldog connector.

Claw-plate connectors consist of metal plates with teeth which are forced into the timber by a bolt and nut. They can be used to join wood to metal or wood to wood.

Shear plates are flush fitting with margins which are recessed into the timber to take the plates, a rim protruding on both sides.

In early wood constructions a basic joinery method of making joists was used for both flooring and roofing, but methods of engineering were later introduced to create stronger joints. The earliest joints were of wood, but metal was found to be more reliable. The basic differences between the two types of

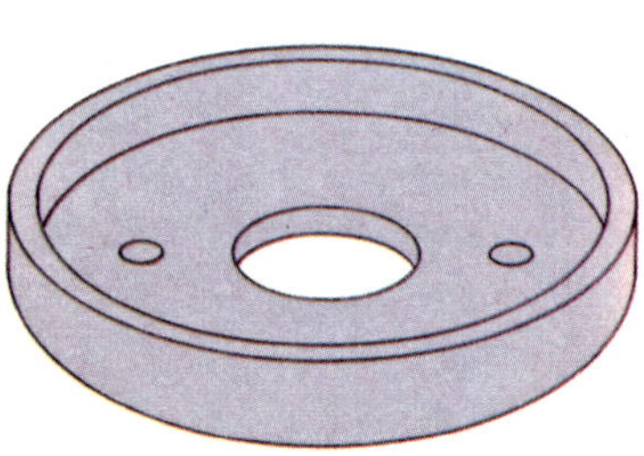

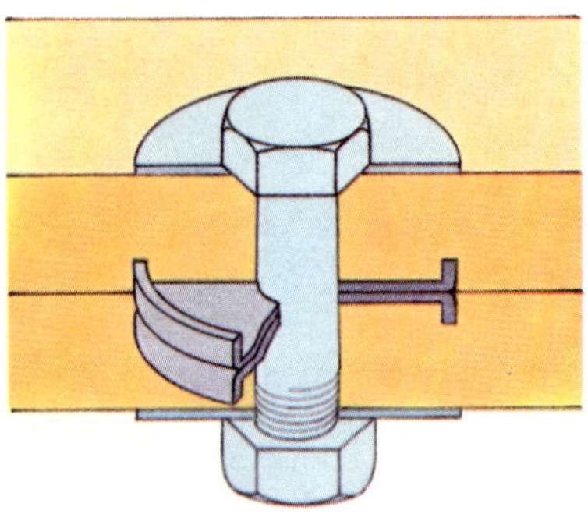

▲ **Shear-plate connectors** are designed for making timber-to-steel unions. They are bedded into recesses in the timber to provide a flush surface.

timber connectors is that the split ring takes the load on the teeth, whereas the claw and shear plates each have a central bolt for load bearing. The advantages of using these connectors when compared with conventional joinery are efficiency, easy fitting, minimum preparation, adaptability.

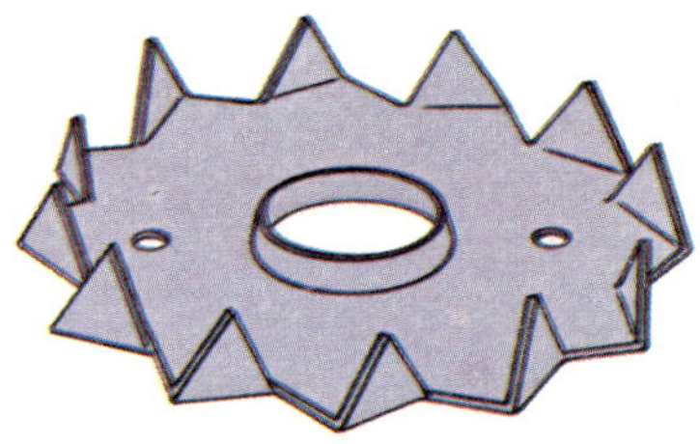

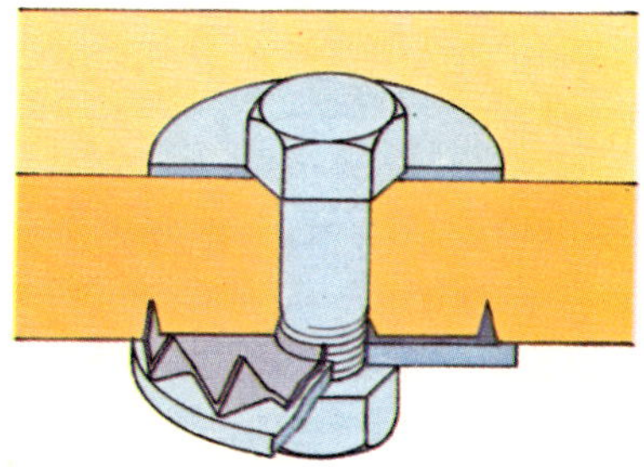

▲ **Circular toothed-plate connectors** can be used to avoid the overlapping of two pieces of timber. In some cases it is possible to effect a joint which is stronger than conventional methods, and this connector can be used for timber-to-timber jointing as well as timber-to-metal.

Adhesives

Synthetic resins are now widely used in the timber construction industry, and many pieces of furniture and even sections of buildings are stuck together with them. They also reinforce the use of metal connectors. Synthetic resins are classed as engineering materials because they play a major role in construction.

The earliest use of adhesives was in 1793, when wood-working machinery to produce veneers was invented. The animal glues originally used have passed out of fashion because synthetic resins which require a force of between 34 and 36 tonnes per centimetre^2 (85 and 90 tons per square inch) to break are freely available. Timber adhesives of this type qualify for use when they have a higher breaking point than the material on which they are used. When pieces of timber are bonded together, the surfaces must be completely smooth and flush to avoid air pockets, which cause a weakening of the bond, and only the thinnest possible adhesive film must be used.

Casein is made from skimmed milk with a protein to form the adhesive. With the addition of formaldehyde and urea, and compounds of sodium and calcium hydroxides, copper and sodium silicate, adhesion can be improved. The enemy of casein is dampness, but the adhesive is useful for internal application, and may be used for panel fastening and in the manufacture of light furniture.

Starch glues are made from cassava starch, caustic soda and water with various additives. Their effectiveness can be impaired by dampness.

Synthetic resins come in many varieties. Compounds of phenolic and urea formaldehydes are used for large-scale bonding, and they require both pressure and heat to cure or harden. The introduction of resins has resulted in the rapid growth of a new industry to utilize the by-products of the saw-mill. Blockboard and laminates are just two examples based on the bonding together, or "welding", of often disparate materials.

Another use of resins is the strengthening of timber by total impregnation of the material to reinforce the cellular fabric by several thousand per cent. It can be done by total immersion or injection, depending on the size of the piece to be treated. With the combined use of connectors and resins and a fund of knowledge about the properties of different timbers, it is now possible to construct large all-timber buildings in such a way as to ensure a life of 60 or more years with a minimum of maintenance, regardless of climate and other extreme conditions.

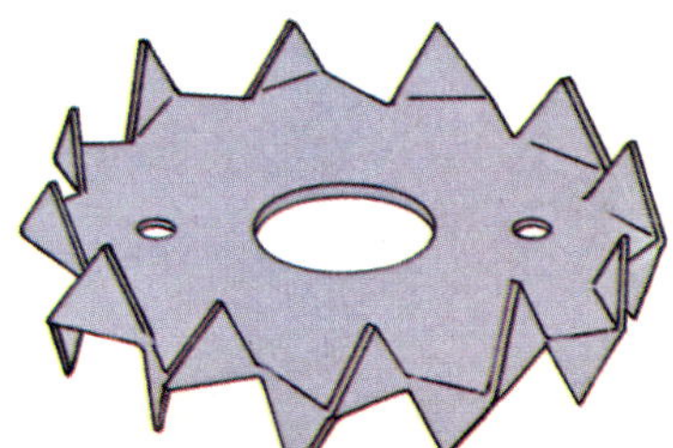

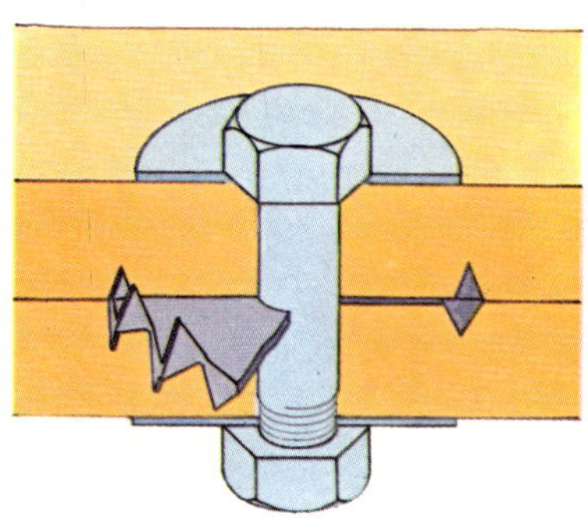

▲ **Claw-plate connectors,** male and female, are used in conjunction with the nut and bolt to pass through the two pieces of timber, and, by tightening the nut, a flush connection is achieved.

Timber housing

Timber housing does not simply mean building a dwelling or any other form of accommodation, such as farm outhouses or leisure chalets, from start to finish on site. Nor does it mean that truckloads of timber are brought to the site in plank form and then cut to size and assembled from the ground up by joiners and carpenters.

▲ Pre-constructed plywood sections, made on-site or off-site, can be assembled into houses very quickly.

Design

While some countries have made better technological progress than others, it is now generally recognized that the use of timber calls for drawing-board design by a special breed of architect, and the co-design of standard fastenings and other fixtures, most of which can be used by unskilled or semi-skilled labour. The all-wood prefabricated house has to be architect-designed by people who have made a sound study of, and have an interest in, the nature of the materials, including their properties and performance in contrasting climates and extremes of temperature. Other study areas include the preservation of the building material over economic periods of time, the amount of stress they are able to bear, and methods of rapidly making and assembling units.

Construction

In recent years it has become possible to build much larger units than before, then move them with custom-designed transporters. The new type of vehicle can carry what amounts to half a house and then offload it on to a prepared foundation, using only the manpower of the driver, his mate and a couple of labourers. In comparison with conventional house building, which is often hampered by adverse weather, the advantages are obvious. They include less manpower, rapid and efficient building systems and the provision of a house which is much less complicated than the ordinary brick, wood and steel construction.

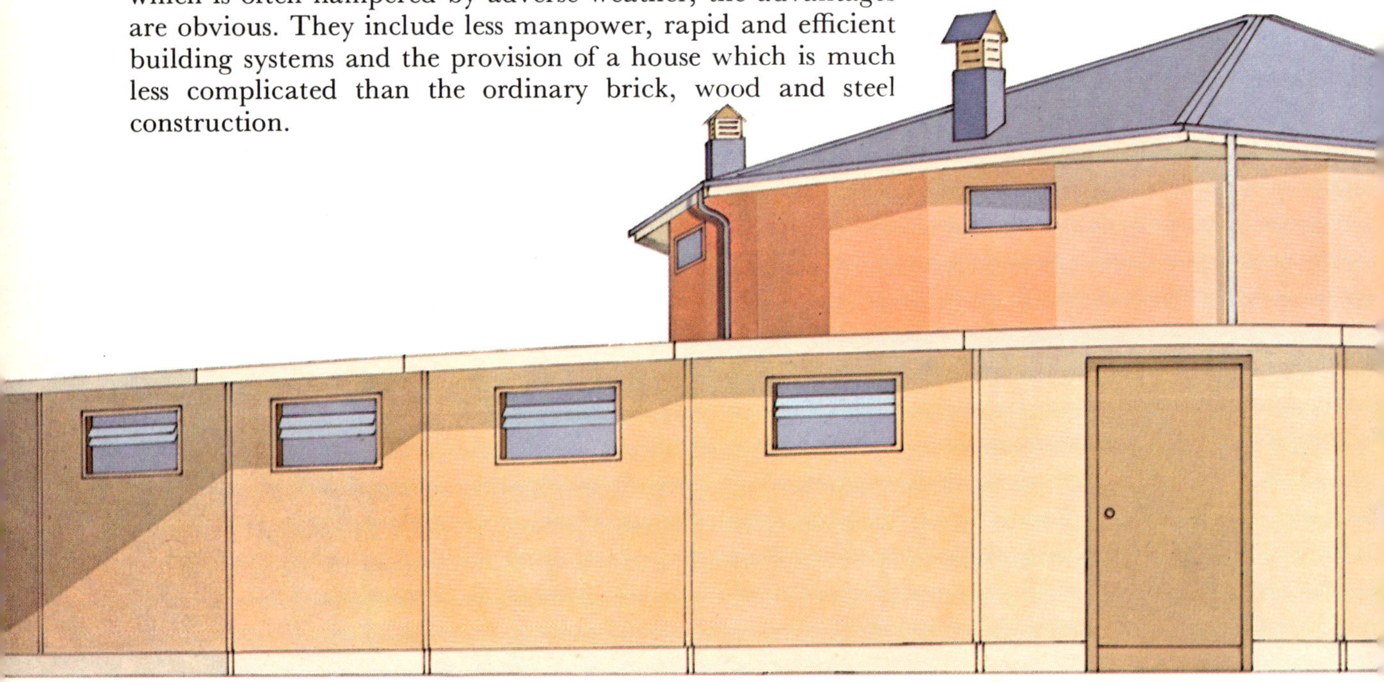

A new kind of stressed-skin housing has been tested against all known hazards, including fire, explosion and implosion, and structural collapse if more units are added to create a taller building. It is possible that multi-family units could be housed in inter-connected groups of units in areas where land use is restricted or the areas happen to be irregular. The stressed skin can be painted or left as it is. As far as the exterior is concerned, it can be used for almost any kind of cladding, such as bricks, tiles or decorative cedar shingles.

▲ This all-timber American house was sawn in half before being transported.

Fire risk

One of the traditional and demonstrably ill-founded prejudices against timber housing from the mortgage and insurance points of view is that wood is more combustible than metal and brick. Tests carried out in Britain have shown that a 30cm^2 (12in square) of European redwood, 3m (10ft) long and capable of carrying a 90 tonne (90 ton) load, has a fire resistance of about 45 minutes, whereas a steel column made to carry the same load will fail in 15 minutes due to softening and distortion. The more dense the timber, the slower it is to char. Experiments are being carried out to find out whether it would be useful to encase steel beams in hardwood "boxes" as a fire precaution in conventional buildings. In the manufacture of wooden houses the use of hardwoods from such areas as West Africa and the Far East is obviously desirable, particularly when it comes to the flooring and internal walls, which may have to confine a fire.

World scene

Countries in which timber housing has been common for many years include Scandinavia, the United States, Canada, where timber is plentiful, and New Zealand and Australia, both of which have a wealth of timber.

In other parts of the world it is still early days. Here and there progress is comparatively slow due to an imbalance of materials production and a lack of coordination between different sectors of the building industry and government housing policies.

▼ This one-off house was architect-designed and built in an exposed site in Canada, using plywood to exploit the insulating and bracing qualities of the material. Expert attention was given to the exterior chemical finish of the panels to ensure long life and still present an attractive appearance. The same techniques are now being used in the building of industrial premises, schools and club and sport pavilions.

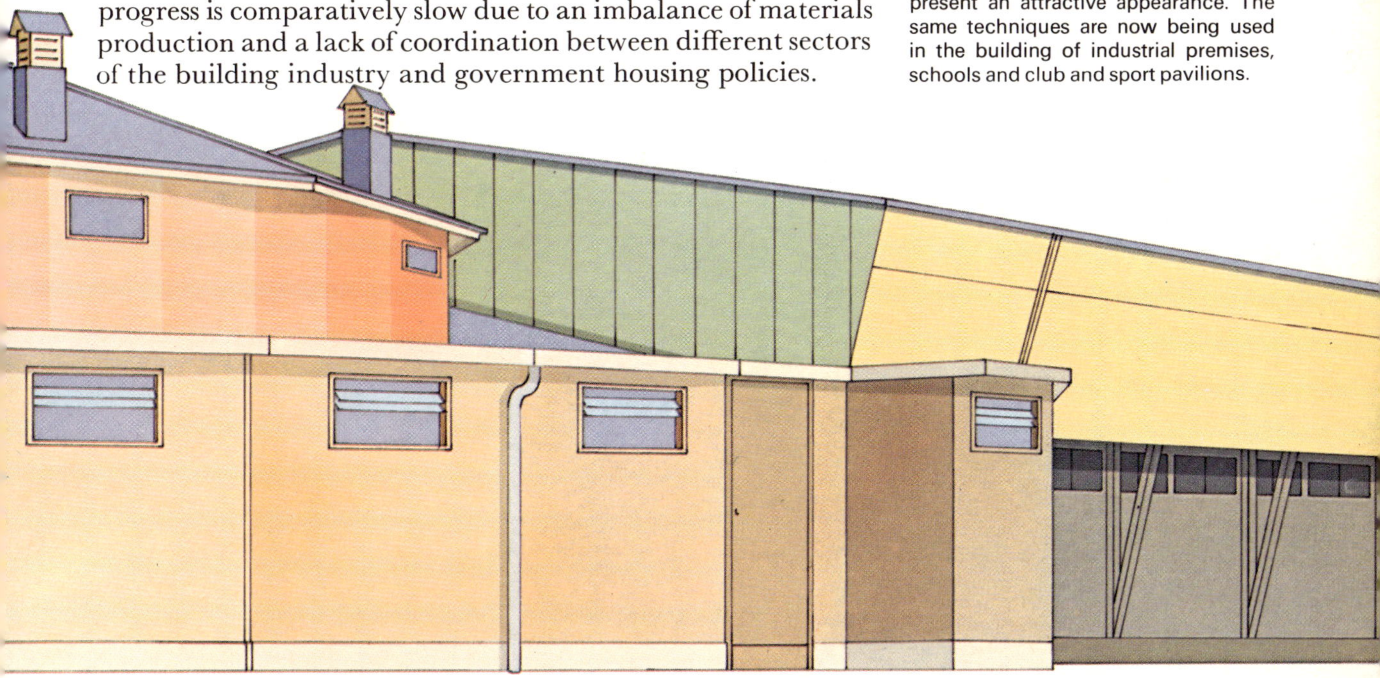

The router

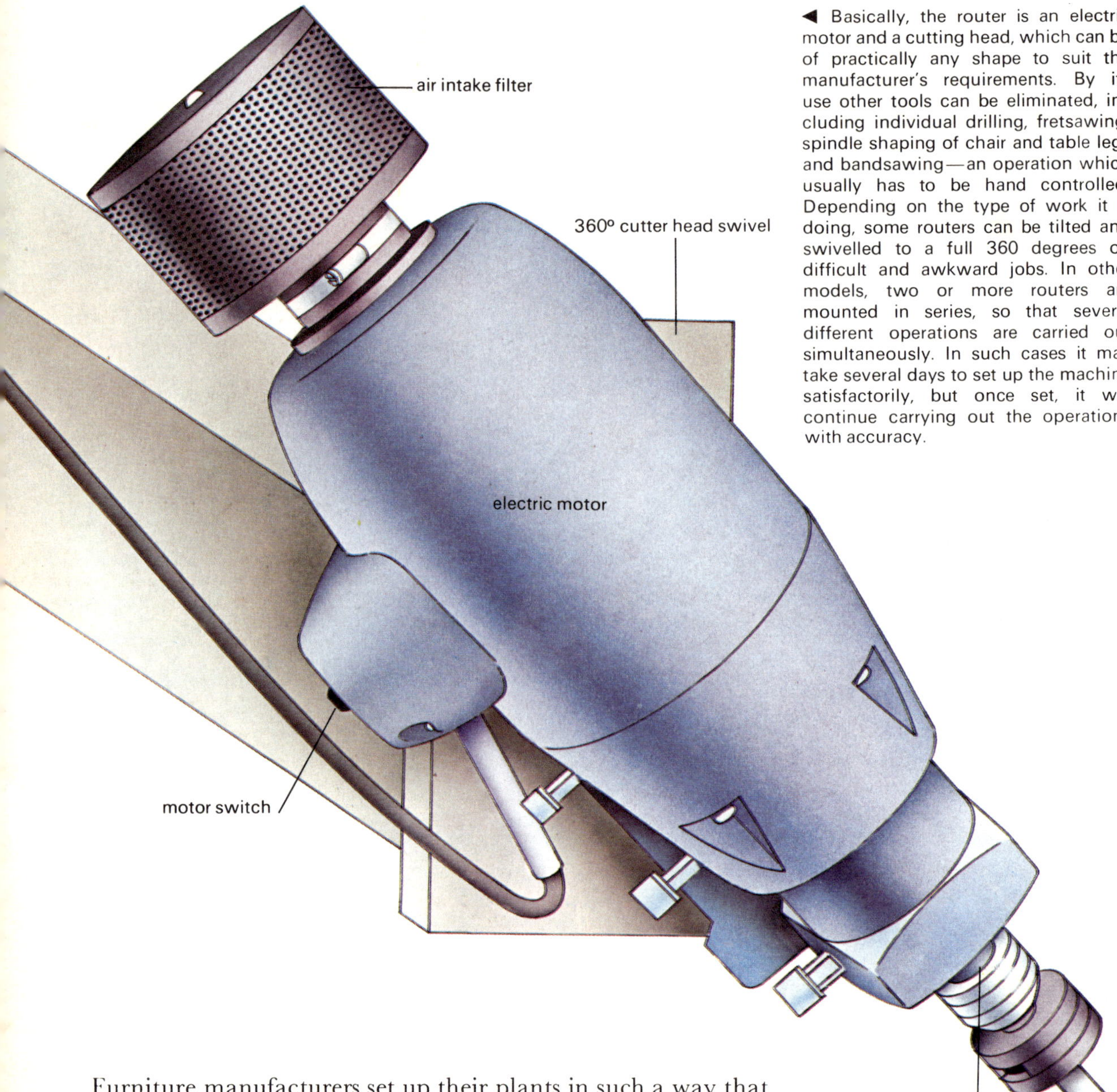

◄ Basically, the router is an electric motor and a cutting head, which can be of practically any shape to suit the manufacturer's requirements. By its use other tools can be eliminated, including individual drilling, fretsawing, spindle shaping of chair and table legs and bandsawing—an operation which usually has to be hand controlled. Depending on the type of work it is doing, some routers can be tilted and swivelled to a full 360 degrees on difficult and awkward jobs. In other models, two or more routers are mounted in series, so that several different operations are carried out simultaneously. In such cases it may take several days to set up the machine satisfactorily, but once set, it will continue carrying out the operations with accuracy.

Furniture manufacturers set up their plants in such a way that they are able to economically and profitably produce a certain number of pieces of furniture within a certain time, each piece being identical with the next. They employ designers to create shapes likely to appeal to the market, they employ experts to explore methods of assembling the separate pieces which go to make up a piece of furniture, and they also consult machining specialists. Machining specialists are a group of people who can either design the machinery or may, in turn, consult machinery manufacturers, who will make the pieces of equipment to produce the component parts of the furniture. At each stage speed and guaranteed precision are required.

Control

Wood machining is the core of production. If it can be partly or wholly automated, so much the better, because this reduces the number of people needed to handle the raw timber. In some cases all that is needed is operators at either end of the production line to control the machinery. In some cases machine minders and quality-control inspectors are stationed at intermediate stages to random check that any particular piece in a batch is accurate.

Apart from pieces being sawn to size before they enter the production line, the most common operation is the use of the router during the passage of the piece through the production line.

"Routing" means accurate, high-speed cutting, shaping and drilling of timber. There are about 14 different types of router, all of them driven by electric motor direct-drive units operating as a rule at 12,000, 18,000 or 24,000 rev./min.

In the typical operation there is a very high throughput of work, because the machine does not require any intervention by the operator, and the wood, providing it is able to reach the router in a correct position, will be drilled or shaped to exact tolerances.

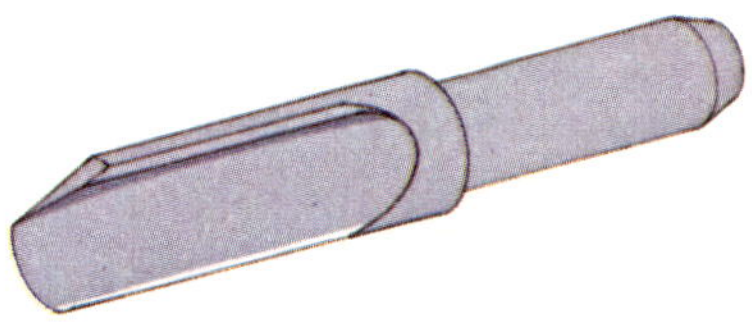

▲ Concentric cutters giving a sharp, reliable cut at high speeds.

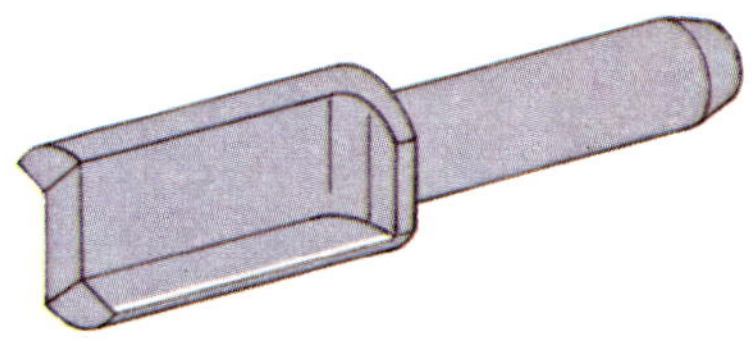

▲ Double-edged cutters designed to throw out the wood chips.

Cutting head

The most important part of the router is the cutting head. With its high-speed operation, the router produces a large volume of wood chips. There are systems to clear these quickly to avoid the machine becoming choked, which may result in the wood being charred and even starting a fire.

Regardless of the shape of the cutting head, only one edge will actually do the cutting. It has been found that when more than one cutting edge is used, the work area becomes choked, causing overheating and premature blunting. As removal of the cutting head for resharpening can cause delays and uneconomic operation of the production line, most manufacturers break down the routing so that several different routers carry out what is ostensibly a single operation. The cutters themselves are designed so that they are sharpened only on the inside face, which permits a large number of resharpening operations. Designers also have to take into account the angle at which the cutter is used. The best cutting angle is 45 degrees.

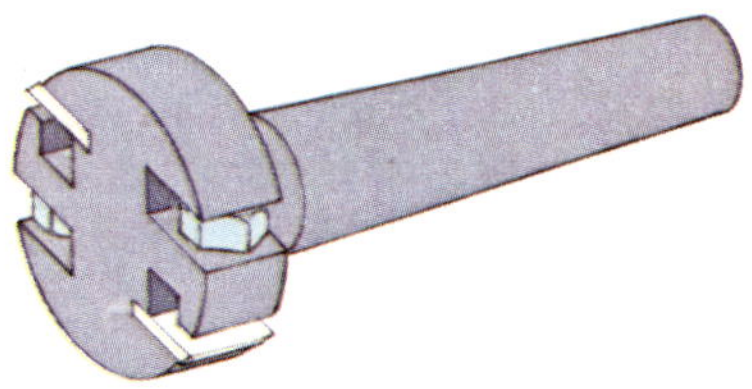

▲ Flat-knife chuck with knives designed for quick cutting.

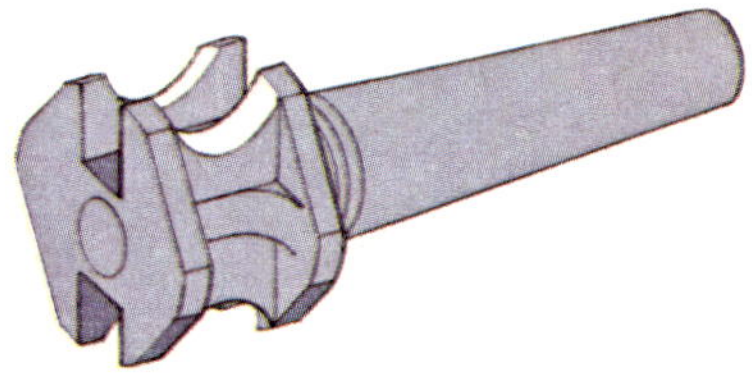

▲ Cutter made for a special job—any shape can be made.

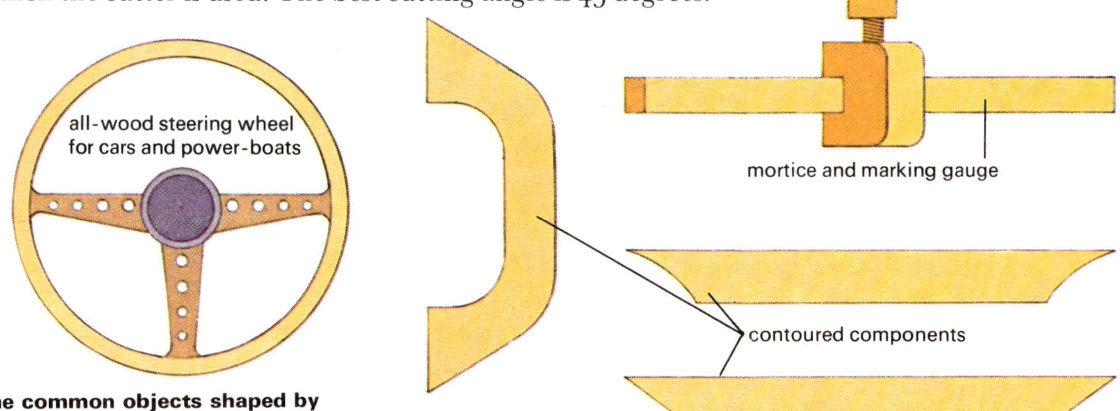

Some common objects shaped by routing.

Saws, planers and lathes

Depending on the size and the scope of the woodworking factory, the planner will install an all-purpose system of separate or combined-function machines located in such a way that the work-pieces can be moved rapidly either by an overhead conveyor or by forklift truck from one machine to another. Alternatively the planner will go for the "all-in" process line through which the timber is fed to emerge at the other end in a completed form. Comparatively few manufacturers, with the exception of those in the mass international market, can afford to have an automated process line installed, and so the majority choose independent machinery units, each one of which can do several jobs. In this way they minimize capital outlay and still retain the essential flexibility which enables them to control the throughput of individual machines and the demands of the market.

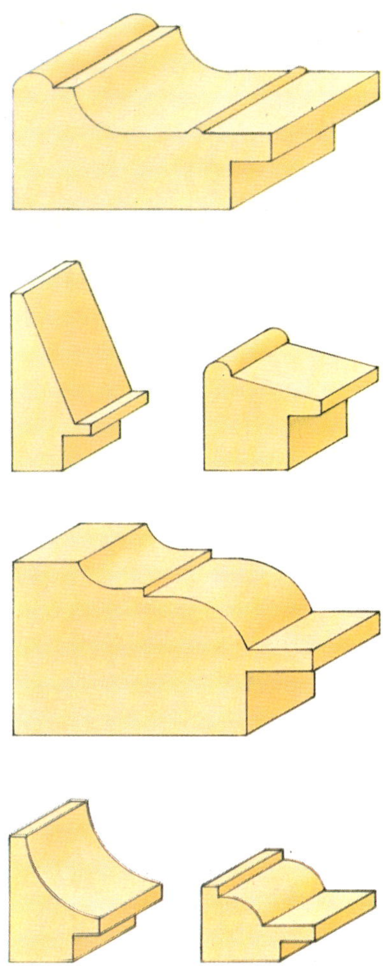

▲ These and many other shapes can be cut automatically on a single machine once the tool bits have been positioned. This fast-working process can produce several hundred battens, joint sections or slotted sections every hour.

Woodturning

Wood turning is the process of shaping the wood as it turns on a central axis. It is an ancient craft and is still done as a handcraft in some places. The first lathes were treadle-driven, but the modern version, equipped with a governor to provide speeds from 400 to 2000 rev./min., can tackle all kinds of wood. This type of lathe is very much in use in many sections of the industry. Basically, the lathe can produce anything which is round, from wooden discs and bowls to legs and plinths of all types and dimensions.

The limit of the lathe is the distance between the two points to left and right, and the depth to the bed of the machine. Large, round, turning jobs can be end-mounted on a special plate, capacity being limited only by the power of the motor.

◀ One of the biggest wood-turning projects ever attempted—the wreathed columns which support the canopy over the high altar in St Paul's Cathedral, London. The specially selected timber was first bonded in sections to form the 4·5m (15ft) sections, then turned on a giant lathe, and rounded by craftsmen using handtools. The wreath design, visualized originally by Christopher Wren but unrealized at the time of his death, was then done by woodcarvers.

Bandsaws

Bandsaws come in many different sizes and have varying capacities, but the principle is always the same. The long flexible blade runs over two or three wheels, enclosed in the housing, and passes through guides above the worktable. These guides are adjustable, and the limit of the machine is governed only by the "neck", which is the distance from the blade to the narrowest part of the housing. Until recently, the sharpening of the blades was one of the most difficult tasks for machine-maintenance specialists, but there are now machines which can be operated by semi-skilled people.

Planing machines

There are many planing machines in use. The latest enable the operator to plane to a predetermined depth not only the two broadest sides but also the edges, all in one operation. It takes only a few seconds to feed even the roughest piece of timber through the machine, which is equipped with rotary blades. Panels for doors and cabinets are processed at the rate of several dozen an hour. The wood shavings are removed by a vacuum system which sucks up the debris and carries it through a pneumatic system to a central dumping point, where it can be used as fuel or recycled for other purposes, including paper making.

Circular saws

Circular saws are a standard feature of all factories, and they vary only in size, from those with blades measuring six inches up to the large ones which are able to cut straight through logs six feet or more in girth. The action of the blade, which is driven by an electric motor—in this case about 5·5cv (hp)—is one of ripping through the timber. Circular saws are used as a rule for rough work, after which the workpiece passes to other sizing and forming equipment, such as the planer and thicknesser. The designer of woodworking machinery measures the speed of the circular saw at its outer rim and is able by this means to estimate its cutting power. The teeth of the circular saw are complex, and it is necessary to sharpen them in several different stages, but there are now machines which can do this without any danger or error of mis-setting the teeth.

▼ This type of bandsaw will cut configurations of great intricacy in preparation for carving or marrying to other pieces up to a thickness of about 15cm (6in) of hardwood.

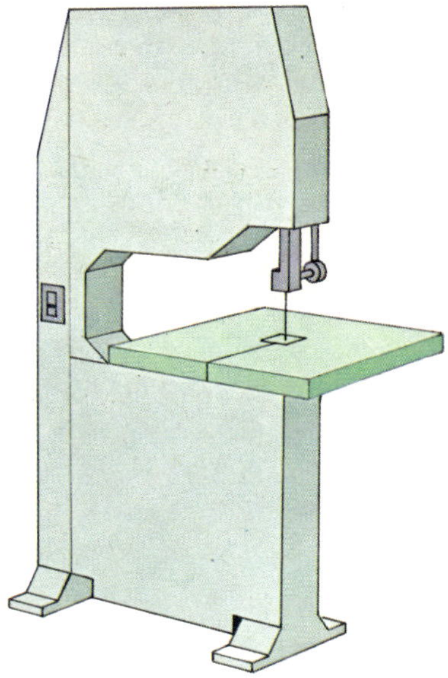

▼ Surface planing and thicknessing is done simultaneously by this machine, which can work at two speeds, depending on the type of wood being processed.

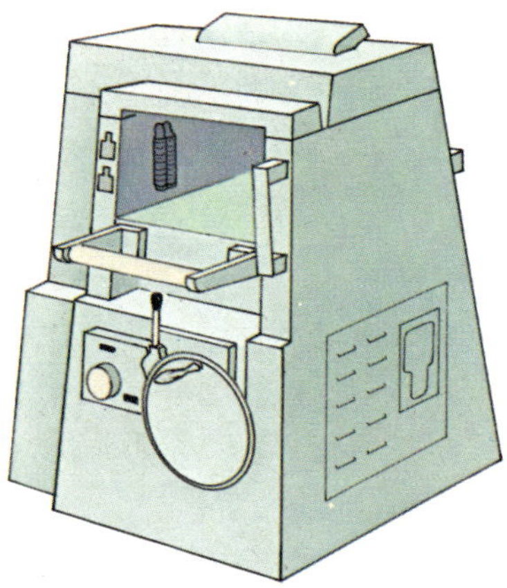

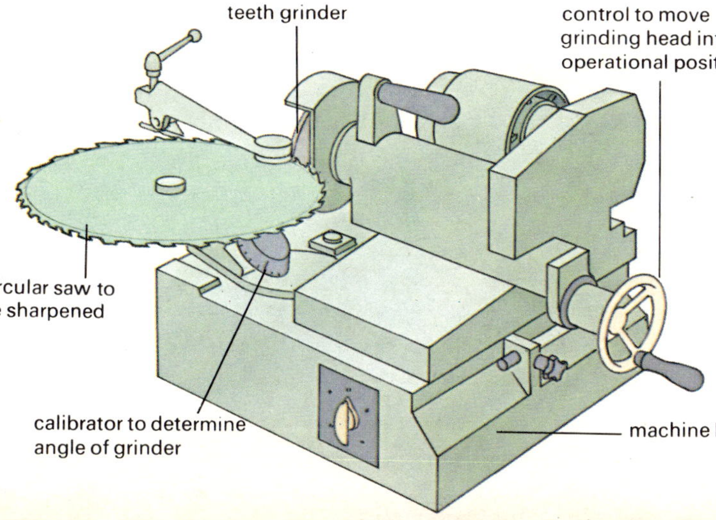

◀ Circular saws need frequent sharpening to remain efficient when cutting all types of timber. This machine makes simple what used to be a lengthy job, because it automatically regrinds the teeth and can be operated by a semi-skilled worker. Relatively low in cost, it saves valuable production time by continuously keeping sets of circular saws sharp and ready for use

The spindle borer

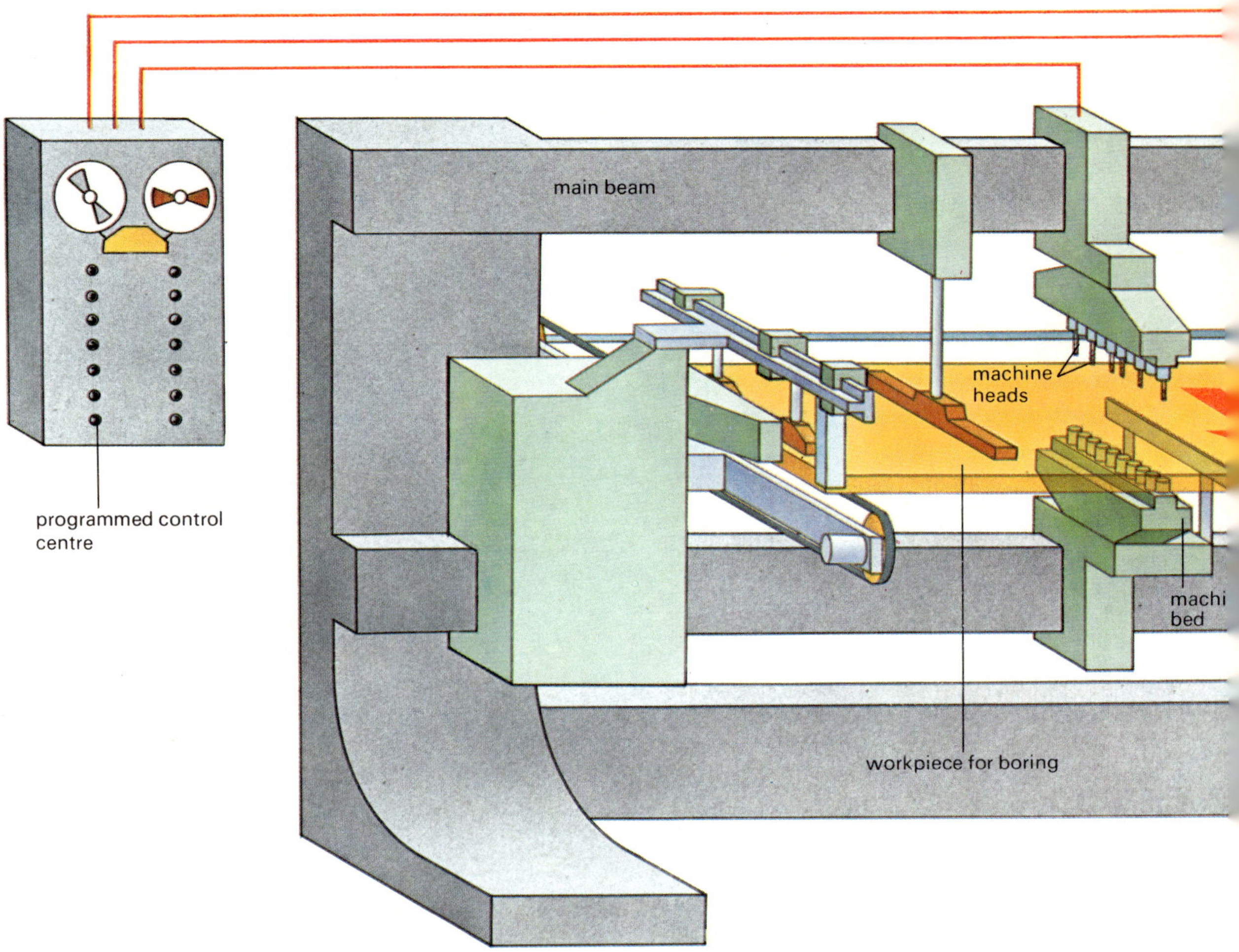

In some instances, the machine can be programmed, transmitting impulses from the electronic section to the mechanical section, adjusting itself automatically to the frequency of delivery of work-pieces from other parts of the assembly line. The total work cycle is about three seconds.

From the economic point of view, a boring machine of this type represents a large investment, but for all its size and apparent complexity, it can be re-tooled to take on a variety of work. The disadvantage is that it cannot handle jobs of a different nature at the same time. Widely used in the furniture industry, it can be incorporated in the fully automated process line, using hydraulics and electricity for its power.

To the left of the machine is the control panel, where the operator can, by pushing the buttons, activate various sections. Although it is used basically for boring holes, it can be used for other operations, and in some versions it has router attachments so that moulding and shaping can be done.

4·5m (15ft) long, it has 2·5cv (hp) motors giving 2800 rev./min. and each of the headstocks, or mountings, carrying up to 20 spindles in which the tools are fixed. With an average of three headstocks, this means that 60 separate boring operations are all carried out at the same time.

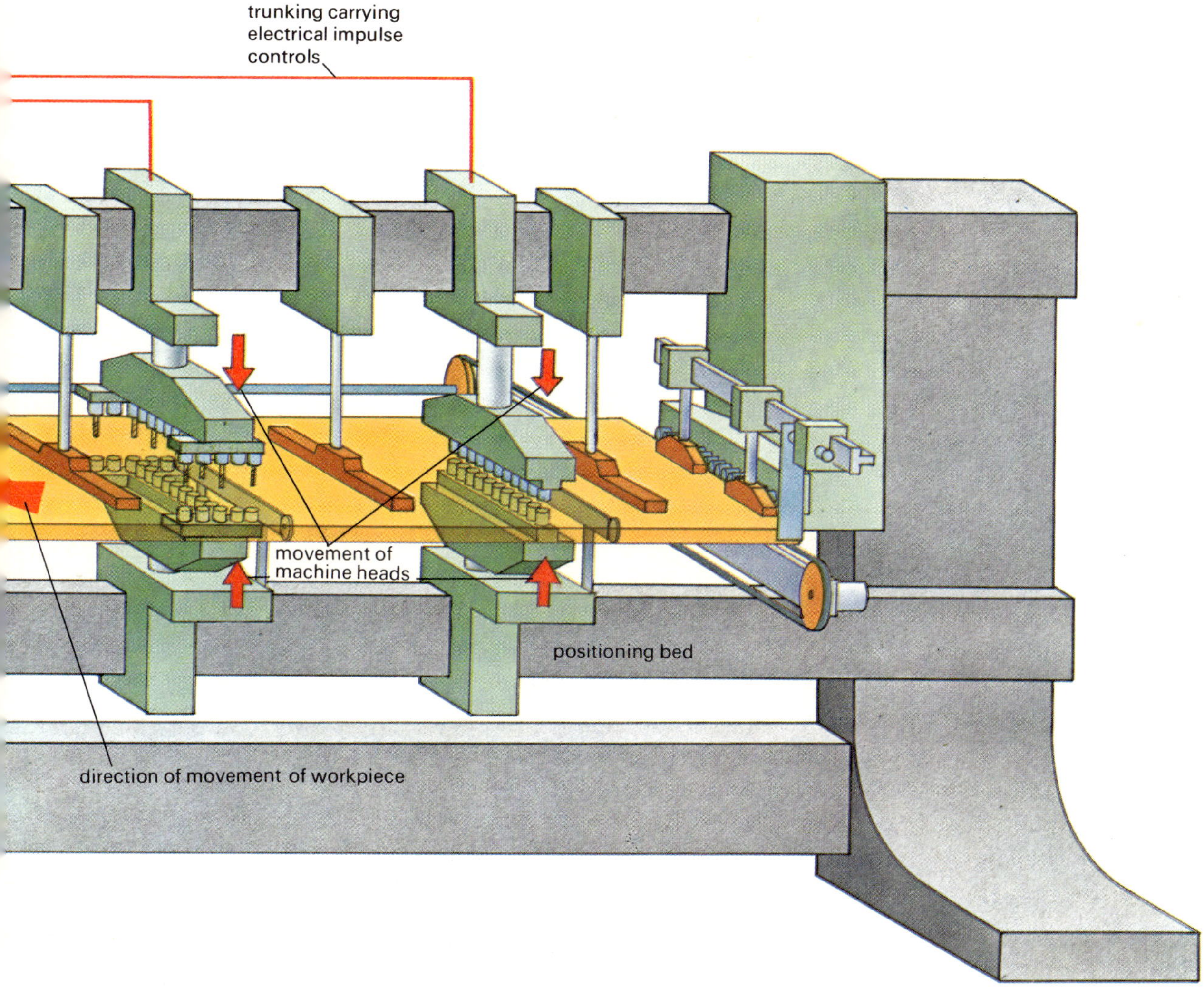

The machine accepts the workpiece and positions it automatically, carries out its work operations, and the heads return to a resting position without any further action by the operator. The conveyor track then starts again to remove the workpiece and accept the next one.

► Drill bits are shorter than in the conventional brace and bit, because the speed of the operation of the machine can create metal fatigue. This is lessened by shortening the shank and using a sleeve-type fitting with a slot and two screws to hold it firm.

Utilization

All kinds of African hardwoods can be used for a variety of purposes in different and often radically opposing climates. Piers, wharfs and jetties, for instance, can be constructed with timber which has been specially treated to withstand marine life, although some sea organisms, such as limpets, may act as reinforcers when they cluster thickly on the timber below the waterline. Many English piers are up to a century old and have required little maintenance, and they were built partly of oak and partly of softwoods.

Fencing

One of the major uses of timber is as fencing. In Britain practically every locality has its own way of fashioning a fence, dictated sometimes by the nature and the properties of the available material, and sometimes by craft traditions in that area. Much depends on the function of the fence itself. For instance, in Lincolnshire hedges are grown round plashing stakes, and in the same county oak or larch are used to last a lifetime on agricultural estates. The motorway-building programme called for hundreds of kilometres of fencing to a strict government-approved specification. On ground used for horse rearing and the enclosure of foals, a fence with a wide top rail is used.

Car construction

Plywood, which has many uses, has been utilized in the construction of car chassis. One model has been made with 4mm ($\frac{1}{6}$in) and 6mm ($\frac{1}{4}$in) plywood. The principles of the wartime wooden-fuselage Mosquito aircraft were applied in the study of stresses and strains. Not only was the chassis of the car made from plywood, but also the seatbacks, floor, dashboard supports, boot, transmission cover, support for the engine frame, rear-axle tunnel and wheel arch supports. The external surface of the chassis was finished with fibreglass on a plywood core.

Veneer

Properly handled and bonded, veneer can be used for practically any kind of construction. One firm has even made a coffee percolator out of it, and then boiled water continuously for 72 hours, using an inner core of plywood. In the main, veneer is used for facing panelling because it is possible to create interesting patterned effects when the figuring is contrasted. Veneer has also been woven to make screens for interior decor, either free-standing or to face walls and staircases, and in one case women's dresses were made from a thinly-sliced veneer, again utilizing the natural patterns, and bonding the veneer to a fabric base to enable the wearer to walk naturally.

▼ Timber pit props have been used from the earliest times, and balks of timber are said to have been used by the builders of the Egyptian pyramids, who transported stone on timber rafts. Many mines which were worked out over a hundred years ago still have their timber roof supports and walls intact, despite the constant seepage of water and the tremendous pressure of earthworks. Although metal rams are now used to put hydraulic roof-jacks into position, timber is still used for pit props. Both hardwoods and softwoods are used for mining and tunnelling work, which nowadays consists mainly of lining deep shafts.

▼ Timber for piers, jetties and wharfs was originally selected to match the schooners and square riggers which were themselves timber-built of the same material. The major enemy of timber which may rest in water for many years is the marine boring worm which first attacks the surface and then works its way into the thickest balk. Many marine borers are transported from one part of the world to the other as "passengers" on the bottoms of ships. When timber is used for submerged constructions nowadays it can be coated with fibreglass and iron-bound. They are made in sections prior to location and bedded down in concrete on the river or coastline bed.

▼ Timber has been phased out for railway wagons, and these days metal is used. The original railway wagons were flatbeds on which freight was tied down, and from them evolved the familiar cattle wagon, designed for transporting livestock across country. The life of wooden wagons was up to 50 years without very much maintenance. They were designed to ride on metal bogeys and chassis with a degree of give and take between the upright walls and roofing.

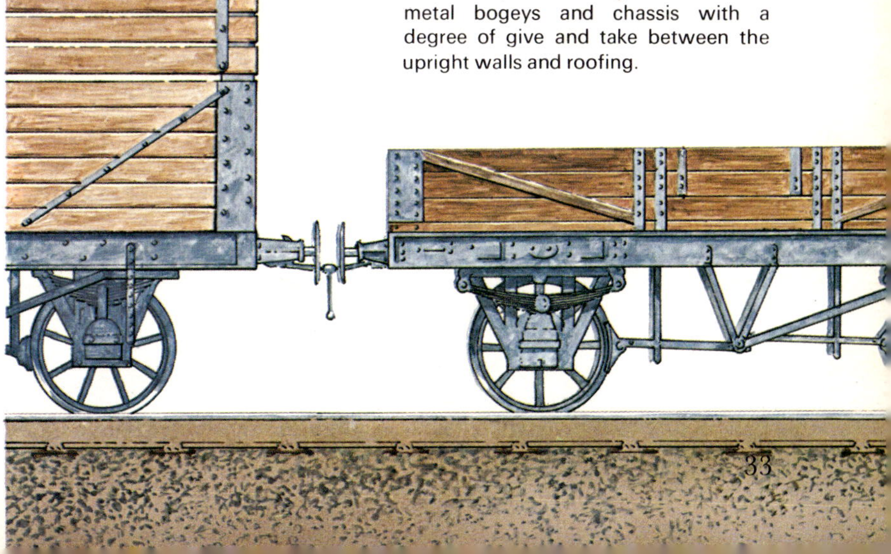

Toys and miniatures

▲ Probably the most famous doll's house in the world was made by a Liverpool craftsman, Ashcroft, for a Miss A. Barton in 1887, and many years later bought by Queen Mary. It is among the most perfect examples of doll's house furnishing.

Ever since wood was found to have a use, people have amused themselves by making miniatures, from dolls for children to scale models of buildings. In the United States one association of woodcarvers has more than 10,000 members throughout the world, many of them accomplished whittlers of intricate objects, such as wooden chains containing wooden spheres in cages, keys and animals.

Miniatures

Japan and China have contributed many miniatures, including the tanagram, which was the ancestor of the jigsaw puzzle. The tanagram consists of only seven pieces, all cut to geometric patterns. The aim is to form them into a square without any edges overlapping.

From India came the six-stick, or cane, puzzle. Six pieces of cane are cut to the same length, each with notches, the puzzle is to fit them together in a star design.

Fans have been whittled from single blocks of wood, some in double or even treble circles, including elaborately carved bases. An American whittler recently produced a complete set of kitchen utensils, each carved out of a single piece of wood, incorporating joints and pivots, all of which worked. Another carved seven pairs of pliers, all joined together and, once more, carved out of a single block of wood. Nowadays, although model kits are available in which the preformed pieces are simply stuck together and then painted, many whittlers continue to produce exhibits, including a miniature theatre containing 30,000 separate pieces. One man carved every piece of a clock, including the movement, with 30 miniature dials, each of which gave the time in the world's capitals.

▲ Before the toy-making industry was organized, fathers used to spend their spare time carving miniature shops for their children, which were handed down from generation to generation. This butcher's shop was carved in about 1840.

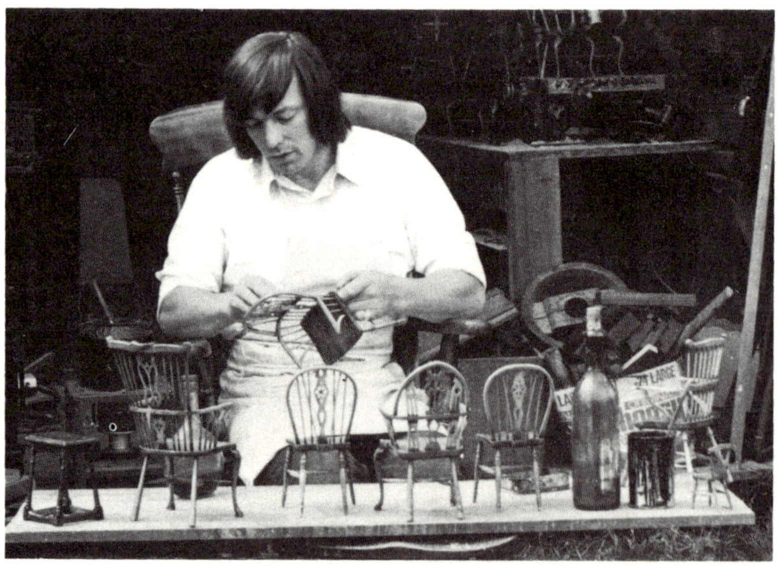

► High Wycombe, Britain, is a traditional furniture-making centre, famous for several centuries for its chair makers. Apart from the perfectly scaled miniatures of chairs, travellers used to carry models of different styles when calling on customers. All these are now collector's pieces. Probably the only craftsman still making miniatures of several different types of chair is Stuart King, seen here working.

◀ In Wales it used to be customary for a man to carve a love spoon and present it to his betrothed as a symbol of his serious intentions. Depending on his skill with the whittling knife, the spoon might include chip-carved designs, incised or stamped designs, and be a single or double spoon. He sometimes included a lover's knot and his own initials and those of his beloved.

▲ Italian peasant carving has always featured the horse. In the villages of Tuscany craftsmen first carved the shapes, then other members of the family decorated them. Toy carving has now died out in Italy, but is widely practised in Switzerland.

Chip carving

For decorative purposes miniature carving often incorporates an art known as chip carving, which is done with special knives, usually made from old saw blades. Chip carving was practised as far back as the 17th century, mainly by German craftsmen who wished to decorate cottage furniture, but there was also a strong tradition amongst seamen, who spent their spare time ornamenting sea-chests and presents for their families. The basis of chip carving is geometric, based on the square, triangle and circle. It has its origins in the Pacific, but it is still practised by rural craftsmen in Scandinavia and the United States. In the United Kingdom practically the only vestige of chip carving is found in Welsh love spoons, but modern carvers are often asked to chip carve mouldings as models for plastic mouldings. The timber used is generally walnut or mahogany, holly, apple or maple, all of which are close-grained without any pronounced grain, or figuring. One of the hallmarks of good chip carving is that it should not be precisely geometric. Examples are collected and high prices paid for those which may, to the amateur, look rather crude and imprecise.

▲ The first "sleeping-eye" doll was patented in 1921, but the method of making the head was invented in 1915. The wooden body and limbs were machine-made, then coated with simulated skin to give a life-like appearance. The joints were a development of the cabinet-maker's method of jointing doors on furniture.

Figure carving

Small figure carving is extremely old. In the Pacific masks were carved and painted, the American Indians carved totem poles, and in many tribes the carver was considered to be someone apart when fashioning religious figures. In the 19th century in Britain there was a vogue for wooden dolls with movable limbs. The tradition continues with dolls made from ordinary wooden clothes pegs, some of which are now becoming collector's items rather than playthings. At the State Carving School at Oberamaggau and the Swiss State Woodcarving School at Briez students spend up to seven years learning how to carve not only small human figures but also animal forms.

Wood by-products

Chipboard and blockboard, which are evenly-textured materials, are made mainly from wood chips and other substances, including wood blocks, bonded together to make a material which can be used for panelling and in cases where large areas have to be covered economically. Some board is made with a surface ready for painting, others are textured, and a variety of types have plastic laminates bonded to them so that they can be shaped by sawing or routing and used without further preparation.

▲ **Five-ply** means that five layers of veneer are glued together and flattened under pressure. The plies are laid in opposite directions for strength and flexibility.

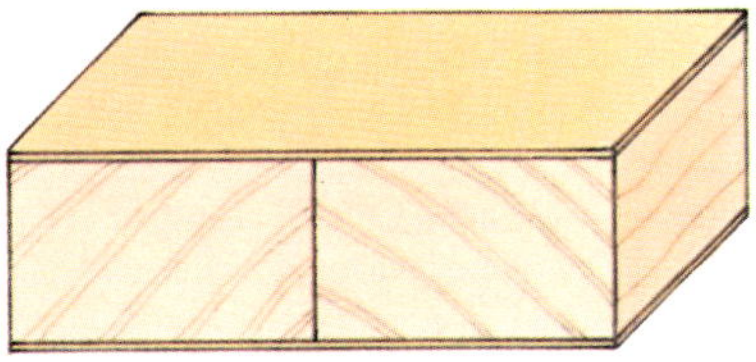

▲ **Blockboard** is made by taking sawn lengths of plywood and facing them with single sheets of thick veneer. The core is placed in such a way as to create inner strength.

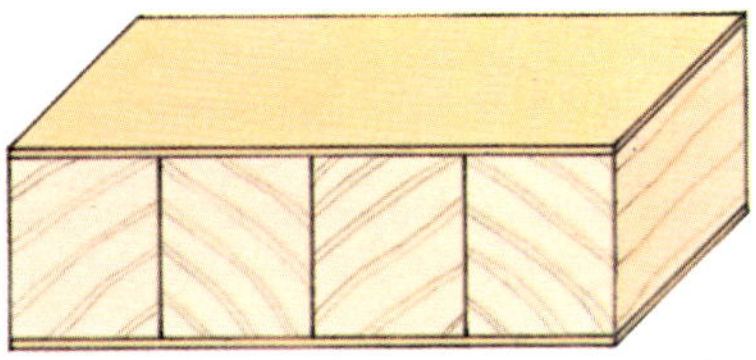

▲ **Battenboard** is a variation of blockboard. It contains relatively wide pieces of blockboard, and is used for major construction work.

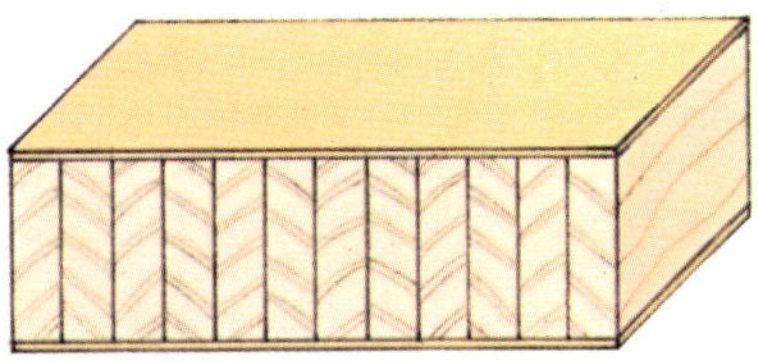

▲ **Laminboard** contains lengths of plywood placed vertical to the top and bottom coverings. It is stronger than blockboard.

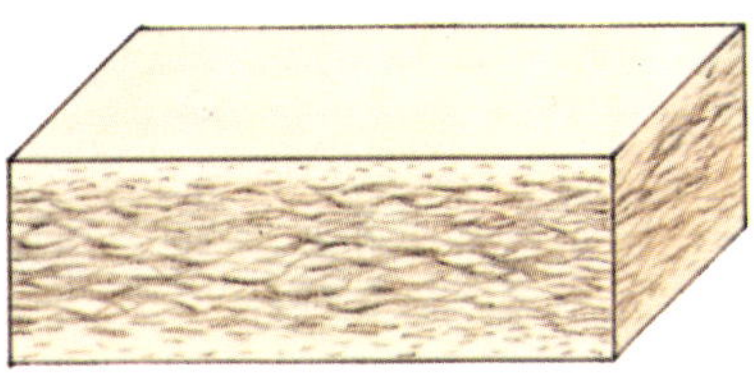

▲ **Chipboard** is a bonded composition of wood shavings which can be sandwiched between veneers and used for such things as mass-produced furniture.

Veneer and plywood

The main by-product of timber is veneer and plywood, the advancement of which has been rapid since 1930, although the bonding of one wood to another has been practised for thousands of years. In 1500 BC the Egyptian craftsmen were adept at marquetry, which consists of glueing contrasting woods to a base for decorative purposes. Little marquetry was practised until the 17th century, which was the result of the invention of machinery for wood cutting. In 1793 a patent was granted to Dr Samuel Bentham for a machine to produce veneers, and this was, in fact, the beginning of the manufacture of plywood. In 1868 an American patent specification included this description: "The invention consists of cementing, or otherwise fastening together, a number of these 'scales' (sheets of veneer) with the grain of the successive pieces, or some of them, running crosswise or diversely from that of others. . . . The crossing or diversification of the grain is of great importance to impart strength and tenacity to the material, protect against splitting, and at the same time preserve it from liability to expansion and contraction." Plywood did not come into general use until 1914, when it was utilized in the furniture-manufacturing industry and for making packing cases.

Adhesives

Other by-products of wood have been made possible by the introduction in recent years of synthetic resin glues, such as phenolic and urea formaldehydes, which require high temperatures and pressures to secure bonding. Other adhesives in use in various industries include formvar, which is derived from polyvinyl alcohol. Blockboard consists of small blocks of wood joined together with these bonding agents. From this has come another development, a glued construction containing laminations, adhesives and connectors. One of the major advantages of this material is that it provides virtually unlimited opportunities for the designer, and it lends itself to the extension of ideas in, for instance, housing, which are at the moment restricted only for want of the materials which can perform to the designer's requirements. This could result in a reduction, or the total abolition, of traditional jointing of timbers.

By-product research

Research into the properties of adhesives is being carried out in all the major wood-using countries. In recent years it has been discovered that certain timbers undergo chemical changes over a period of time which make them unsuitable for bonding. Many veneers which may have been cut several years ago will not bond well, even when the latest adhesives and resin-based bonding agents are used. Investigations have been made into the thickness of the film of glue used on many different woods, and in some cases veneers have been withdrawn from the world market. In more than one major building project, when veneers have cracked, or crazed, it was thought originally that the adhesives, or bonding agents, were at fault, but laboratory research used intensive microscopy and the electron microscope to look into the changes in the molecular structure of the fibres of the timber itself. This has not meant the wholesale withdrawal of all desirable and attractive veneers, but simply a change in the adhesives with the result that those now in use are selected with as much care as the veneer itself to avoid cracking and crazing in a variety of temperatures.

▼ Veneers being matched and joined together in a factory.

▲ Debarking of the rough log continues until the wood proper is reached.

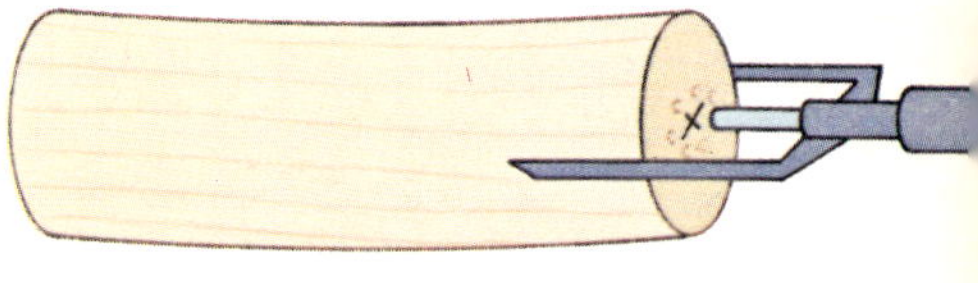

▲ The log is centred and straightened. All irregularities have to be removed until the log is absolutely cylindrical.

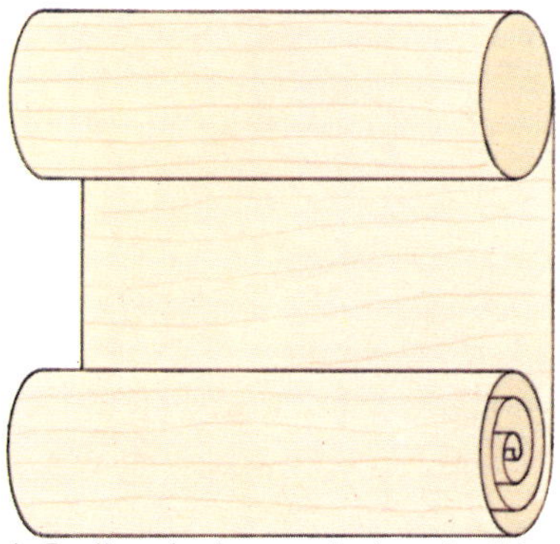

▲ Peeling the log results in a flexible sheet which is then placed in a press to flatten it. Some veneers require special treatment to prevent splitting when dried out.

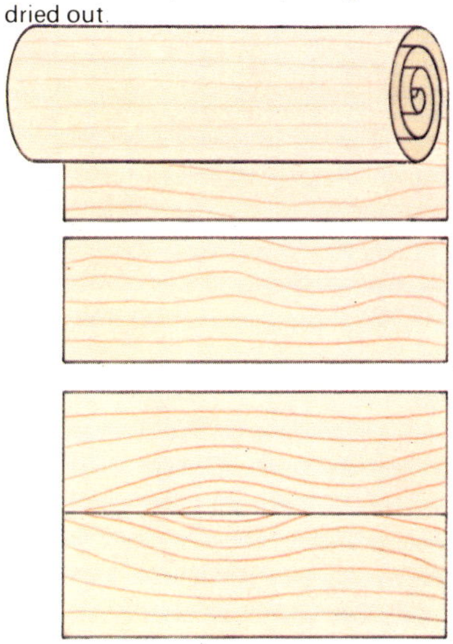

▲ Veneer peels off in a natural sequence, following the natural figuring of the timber, and it is cut and stacked in continuity for users who wish to buy sections which match.

Boat construction

▲ The 19th century clipper "Tapeing" helps to show that the basic shape of the prow has changed very little over the years.

Eleven thousand years ago the Egyptians were using timber to make seagoing vessels driven by sails. In 2900 BC they were constructing ships by fastening together blocks of acacia. Their designs did not include frame or keel, but it is known that the ships travelled long distances across oceans. Since the middle of the last century wood has been overtaken by many materials, the most recent being fibreglass. But even with this relatively developed technology, the master shape of the hull is generally made of wood.

Advantages

In the last few years several advantages have appeared and made timber more attractive to the boat builders. The first is the technique of hot or cold moulding, using many thin wood veneers to build up a skin to a required thickness. The second is the lamination of structural elements, using thinner pieces to create shaped members to fine tolerances. The third advantage is the use of plywood, which can withstand high stresses. In each of these three techniques the new resin adhesives have a part to play in bonding parts together and providing a durable and tough seal.

West African timbers

Research has shown that woods other than the traditional teak, oak and elm can be used. Most of them are West African in origin, and many are able to resist marine boring creatures, which form a traditional hazard of wood when it is immersed in sea water. Boat builders are conservative in their approach to the choice of timbers, and for many years they clung to the idea that oak or yew were preferable for the keel, stern posts, frames and floors. Although part of this opinion was influenced by sheer economics, it has now become apparent that many West African woods are as suitable and in some cases cheaper. They include opepe, afzerlia, danta, ekki and okan.

▼ When it is driven at top speed this patrol boat for use in coastal waters and open seas can reach up to 50 knots. With its main construction of timber, it has to be designed by marine architects who have a full working knowledge of a variety of timbers, because when the keel raises up from the sea and then comes down again with great force, all the timbers are under strain.

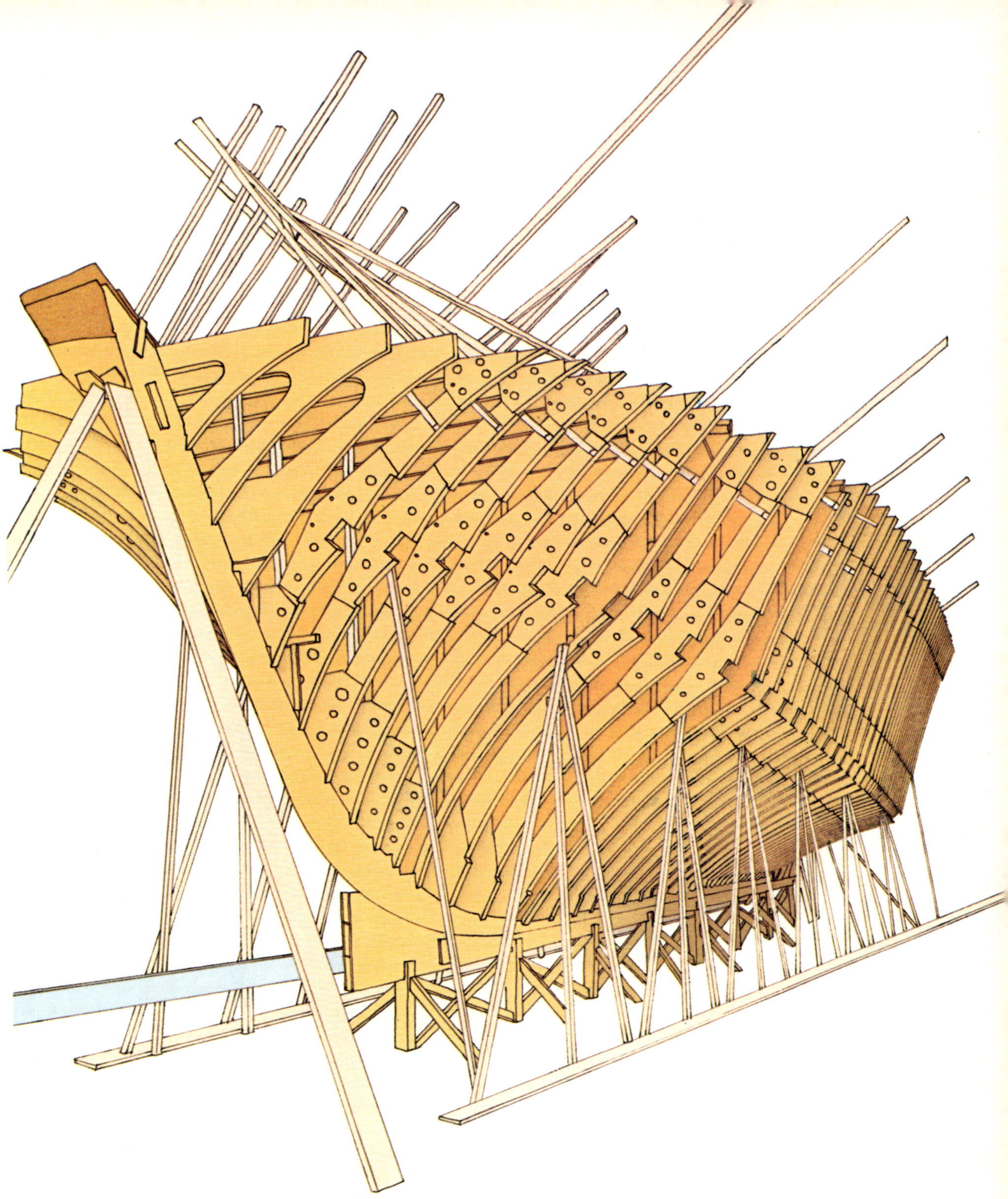

Patrol boat under construction Fast craft like this are being built in Germany, Denmark, Malaysia and Brunei. Cheaper than metal to build, they use specially developed jointing techniques and special glues, but only one main type of glue is used in the entire assembly. Plywood is used for bulkheads, beams and other important dividing sections and both exterior and interior are treated with long-lasting preservative to prevent rotting of wood fibres. Solid timbers are used, including Canadian elm and African mahogany. The timber is supplied to the boatyard in planks which are thin enough to disclose any defects before being used for construction. Depending on which section of the boat is being put together, the planks are bonded together, paying close attention to the ratio of strength and weight. The keel of the craft is made from laminated sections of elm, the stem of similar materials, while reinforcement is provided at strategic points by the use of birch. The longitudinal strength of the craft comes from large bottom girders, which also provide a bedding for the engine. The decking is mahogany, and in boats of under 30m (100ft) it is necessary to have a thickness of only 2·5cm (1in.).

Paper manufacture

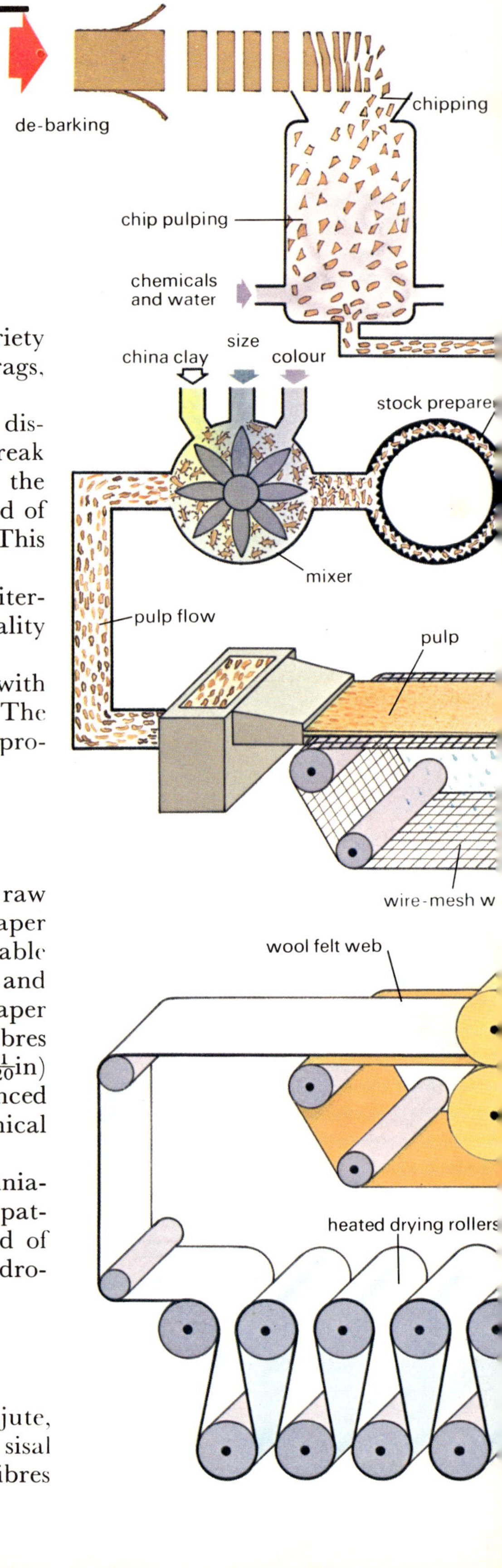

Paper has been made for the last two thousand years. A variety of materials have been used in its manufacture, including rags, straw and nettles.

The possibilities of using wood in paper making were discovered in Germany in 1844. A grindstone was used to break down tree trunks into splinters or groundwood pulp. At the same time Watt and Burgess in Britain invented a method of breaking down wood with caustic soda under pressure. This was called chemical wood pulp.

Other materials were introduced later. In 1861 Mediterranean esparto grass was used in Britain to make high quality printing papers.

Wood as the basis of paper manufacture was increased with the introduction of the sulphite, or bisulphite, process. The advantage of this process over others is that an acidic liquor produces a very clean and white paper with stronger fibres.

Structure of paper

Paper is composed of vegetable fibres. Basically, almost all raw materials, including vegetable fibres, are suitable for paper making, but not all have lasting qualities. After the vegetable fibres have been reduced to pulp, they are rolled out flat and then intermeshed. The factor which determines the paper quality is the structure of the fibres. Microscopically, the fibres are tubes with closed or tapered ends between 1·2mm ($\frac{1}{20}$in) and 3·6mm ($\frac{1}{6}$in) long. Paper strength is directly influenced by fibre strength, and this, in turn, is influenced by the chemical composition of the tree.

Wood fibres contain fibrils which resemble fibres in miniature. When reconstituted after pulping, they re-form to a pattern resembling their original state. Fibrils are composed of cellulose, containing 44·4 per cent carbon, 6·2 per cent hydrogen and 49·4 per cent oxygen, expressed as ($C_6H_{10}O_5$).

Raw materials

Although the main materials include flax, hemp and jute, grass fibres like sugar cane, maize stalks and bamboo, and sisal and esparto leaves, the most vital materials are wood fibres

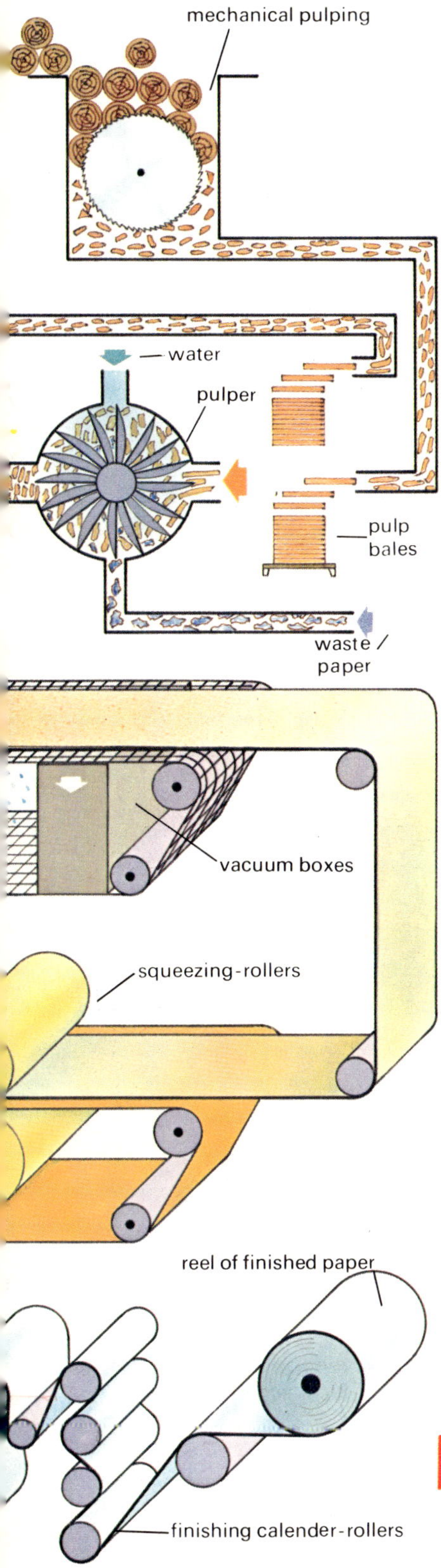

from conifers and deciduous timbers.

Mechanical wood pulp is made from spruce. In quality it is relatively poor in strength and has to be reinforced with chemical wood pulp. The paper is used mainly for newsprint and magazines, and as wrapping paper.

Chemical wood pulp is made from coniferous and deciduous timbers. Conifers have a high resin content, which is dissolved with alkali. Deciduous fibres are isolated by the same method.

Preparation of timber

Spruce is felled in Finland, Sweden, Norway, Canada and the United States in the autumn, the logs are trimmed and floated by river to the mills. After the bark is removed, they are put into revolving drums with large quantities of water. Knots are removed and the logs then pass into grinders, which shred them into fibrous material.

Wet pulp is then passed over perforated screens so that fibres are automatically graded and any lumps rejected. Water is removed so that the pulp can be despatched in one of two conditions, "air dry" which contains 10 per cent moisture, or "wet", containing 45 per cent. One hundred tons of timber can yield between 90 tonnes (tons) and 95 tonnes (tons) of air-dry pulp.

The mixture of pulp is cooked and then washed, and screened to remove impurities, then bleached with hypochlorite or peroxide, and the moisture content removed. When it reaches the mill it is put into a hydrapulper, which disintegrates it by beating in a machine called a potcher. At a later stage it is further beaten and refined at high speed in machines running at 1200 rev./min., using rollers weighing up to 10 tonnes (tons) fitted with blades rotating at 600m (2000ft) per minute.

Additives or fillers

Kaolin, gypsum, titanium dioxide, calcium carbonate, talc and kieselguhr are all used in the manufacture of various types of paper, such as greaseproof, blotting and cigarette papers.

Paper is sized to prevent ink blotting and to waterproof it. The process is known as *engine sizing*, and the main material is rosin, or colophony, a product of the pine. This gummy material is distilled with water, the turpentine content is extracted, and the substance then sets to be reconstituted for use with weak alkali. Sulphate of alumina is added to make it coat the fibres during manufacture.

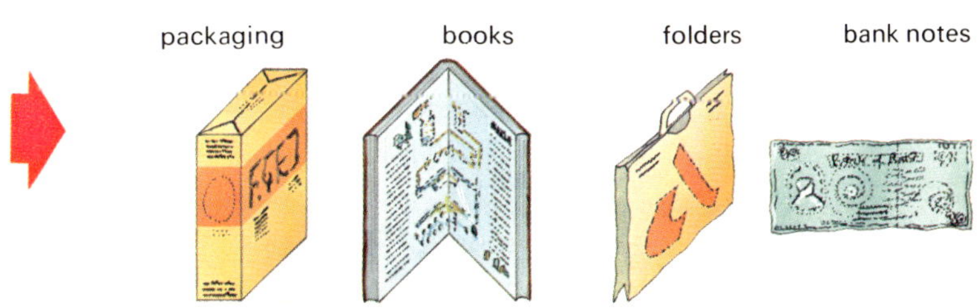

Furniture design

The common chair has been the subject of intensive scientific studies, and it has also been sieved through the mesh of years of research to arrive at the perfect shape to fit the human form. From being a stool with a back fixed to it, the chair has become many things, from thrones for Popes and emperors to the elegance of Hepplewhite and on to the unexpected bean-bag, which is a large plastic-granule filled bag capable of moulding itself to the contours of any sitter.

In its time furniture has been utilitarian and functional, in a heavily ornamented form it has become *objet d'art*, it has been used in both the secular and religious environments, it has been ugly and beautiful. When the great and often over-furnished stately homes of Britain were in their 18th century heyday, village craftsmen were producing smaller copies of the gentry's often massive sideboards, cupboards, chairs and tables for the villagers who wanted to ape the wealthy. Cottage furniture had its own charm, it now reaches high prices in the salerooms. The authentic Welsh dresser is just one example. There are many others.

Aalto

Some of the most striking advances in chair design were made by a Finnish designer, Hugo Alvar Aalto (*b.* 1899). Aalto abandoned conventional joinery and adopted tubular steel, but he later mixed the two media in such a way that laminated birch and ash plywood played their own part in the design. In the 1930s Aalto originated chairs which were the result of a cross-fertilization of ideas, following his study of methods of making skis. The curved and scrolled plywood furniture which he designed in later years resulted in the transition of his shapes to moulded plastic chairs. Aalto, who regarded furniture as "the accessories of architecture", aimed always to create a genre of furniture which was elementary and could be universally applied in any environment.

▼ Ladder-back chair designed by Mackintosh about 1902.

▼ Painted wooden chair designed by Rietveld about 1917.

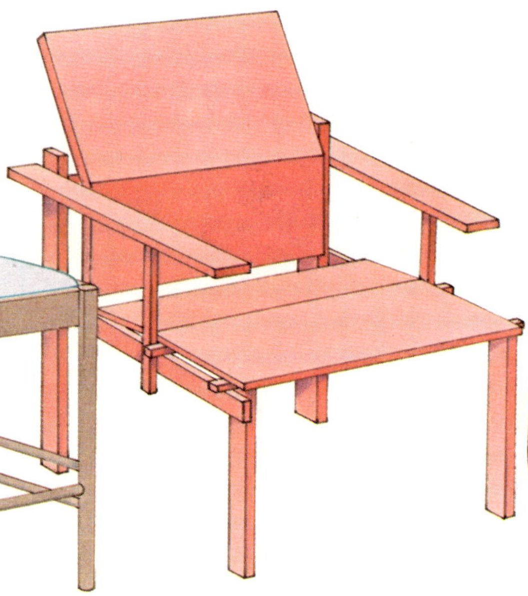

▼ Aalto's plywood cantilever chair, 1935.

▲ The elegant "Nénuphar" writing table of mahogany and gilt bronze mounts designed by Louis Majorelle about 1900.

Rietveld

Starkness of design and clean lines were Gerrit Thomas Rietveld's (1888–1964) hallmark. He served his apprenticeship as the son of a joiner, but rapidly departed from tradition after being smitten by the ideas of the American architect, Frank Lloyd Wright (1869–1959). In 1917 Rietveld produced his first chairs, many of them simply a framework of laths placed at right angles to each other with nothing more than a board seat, a longer board for the back support and two narrow ones for the arms.

Breuer

Marcel Breuer (*b.* 1902) began to design and produce chairs with canvas seats and back-straps. In 1925 he was put in charge of the Bauhaus cabinet-making department, but took more interest in tubular steel furniture than in the use of timber. In 1933 he settled in England as the partner in a firm of architects, and designed a number of laminated bent-birch plywood pieces of furniture, some of them based on Aalto's "ski" chair ideas. One of the criticisms was that he lacked originality, but in the course of his development he did underline the fact that chairs do not necessarily need three or more legs in order to provide adequate support.

Klint

Much more traditional in his approach, but still with a strong influence on the pattern of modern furniture design was Kaare Klint (1888–1954), son of a leading Danish architect. Eschewing the earlier self-conscious folk-appearance of furniture made by many of his contemporaries, he based his studies and those of his students on the far past, because he believed that the wealth of knowledge accumulated by designers over the ages should not be overlooked or discarded at the cost of sheer innovation and novelty. All his work had a beautiful appearance created by a simple waxing and polishing of the bare wood.

Furniture manufacture

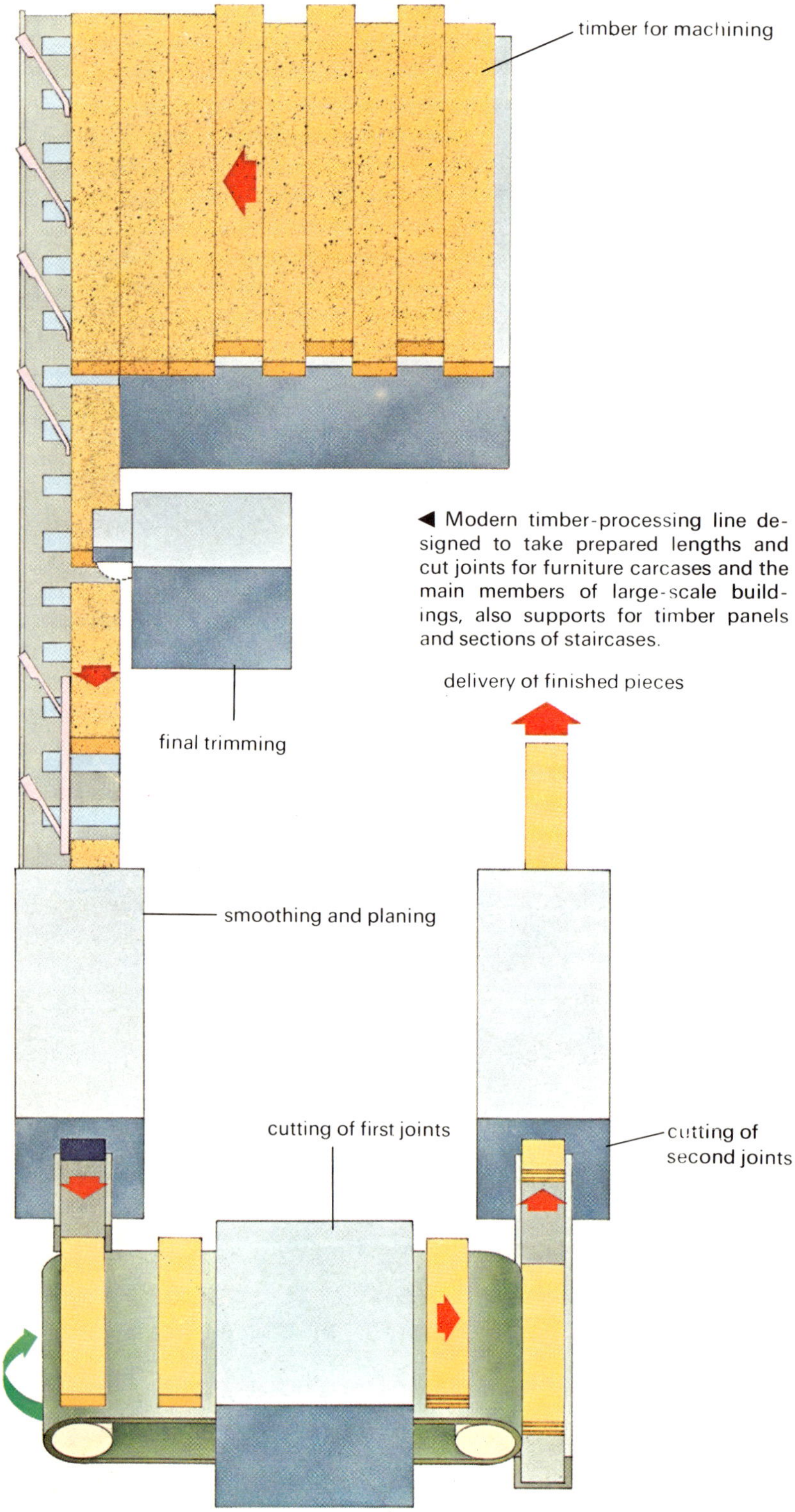

◀ Modern timber-processing line designed to take prepared lengths and cut joints for furniture carcases and the main members of large-scale buildings, also supports for timber panels and sections of staircases.

▲ **Squared length of timber**

▲ **Smoothed and planed**

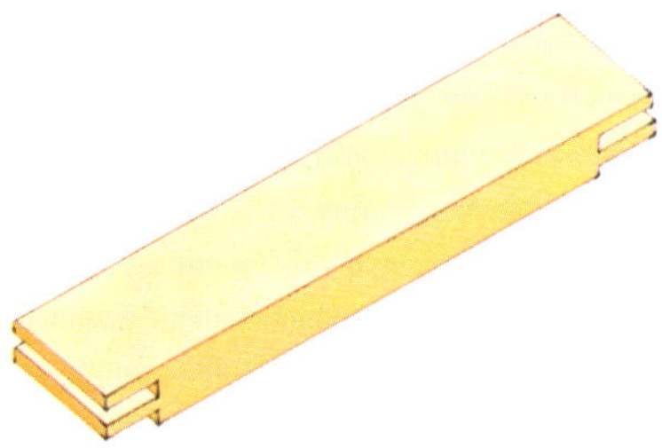

▲ **First joint sections cut to mate with joint below**

▲ **Second joint sections cut to mate with above**

Although many factories are simply assembly points, there are some large plants where the entire process, from taking the seasoned timber from the supplier, to the complete making of furniture and packing for shipment to the wholesaler, is done with the aid of automation. Modern furniture can be made in such a way that its lines are dictated more by the abilities of the automated production line than by any great artistic taste. The craftsman hardly enters into the process, since flat planes and straight lines with only the occasional curve are in current vogue, and much occasional furnishing is not made of wood but of upholstery or synthetic materials on metal frames, or carcases.

New types of furniture

In the 1940s or 1950s, when automation was becoming more widespread and even intricate machine tools were being made without human intervention on the basis of computer programmes which controlled the activities of machines, the furniture industry began to rationalize itself by acknowledging that a new kind of lightweight wooden furniture was desirable. This, in turn, was forced upon the industry by the building of houses with small rooms which could not accommodate the traditional large furniture which had been a standard of design for more than half a century. The day of the "dining suite" and the large bed was over. New houses with their need for as much floor space as could be used, demanded new types of furniture. In some sectors the furniture was prefabricated at the same time as the house itself, the entire unit being made in one factory.

Programmed assembly

Such developments caused the adaptation of automated assembly lines in which the programmed computer could handle what are, after all, very simple geometric shapes at the rate of several hundred or more an hour. Cheap furniture need not be battened and requires only a slight and light carcase on to which plywood can be fastened by synthetic adhesives or tacked, the joints being covered with veneer or synthetic materials.

Automated lines

An automated workline such as this is simply a series of specialized machines which have a connecting link for the handling of the pieces of timber. The link may consist of powered rollers which come into play between each work stage. When the operation has been completed, the piece moves on. Such operations are completed in a fraction of the time it takes to do them by hand, using traditional methods. Planing and thicknessing, for instance, are basically a reducing and smoothing of the timber pieces, and while one side of the workpiece is being cut down the other side may be simultaneously planed. The cutting of joints is done to fine tolerances with sharp chisel-like tools which are replaced on a "planned maintenance" basis. The economic operation of the entire automated line depends on the concept of planned maintenance in which it is known by the operating engineers that certain operational areas will need the replacement of the workheads at intervals. In the large plant two lines may be at work, one being shut down for maintenance while the other continues working.

▶Regardless of the degree of automation some parts of the assembly process are best done manually. Here, chair seats are being added to the chair frames.

Traditional finishing

Ever since timber was first used the surface was painted and embellished with precious and semi-precious stones and metals. Religious figures, furniture, the facades and interiors of both houses and public buildings were covered with pigments and materials of one kind or another. Timber seagoing vessels were treated with many coats of paint on external surfaces which had to withstand extremes of weather. Below decks the timbers were either varnished or scoured and bleached.

Marquetry

During the 17th century the French decorated their furniture with many different kinds of materials, such as ivory, tortoiseshell, brass and even polished or painted tin. In the Italian baroque period a system called *pietra dura*, involving the inlaying of wood surfaces with polished precious stones, was widely practised. From this and earlier and more primitive sources the art of marquetry grew. Marquetry consists of covering wood in patterns with pieces of veneer made from exotic woods.

It is not only the design and lineage of antique furniture that attracts high saleroom prices but also the quality of the surface

◀ This pedestal clock made by Jacques Thuret (1694–1738) has a case decorated with tortoiseshell, bronze plating, and with ornaments in gilt, brass and white metal on a body of oak.

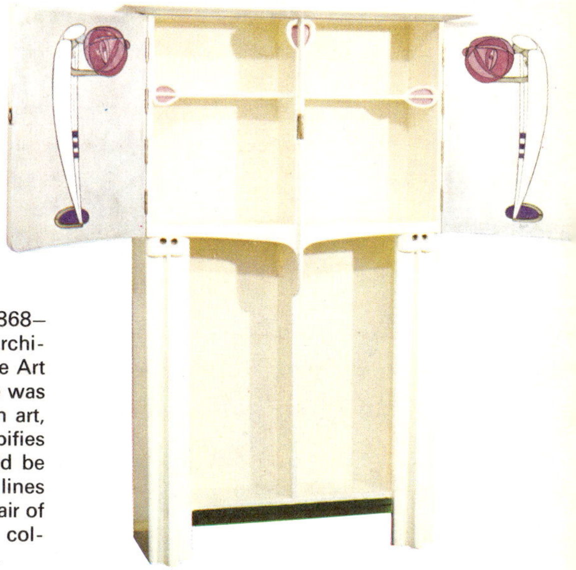

▼ The case of this cembalo—a member of the harpsichord family of musical instruments—was made in 1710, and decorated in the Oriental, or chinoiserie, style, using gilding and rich scarlet for the figure and edge painting. The white background would be executed by a wood finisher, but the delicate figure painting was done by an artist.

▶ Charles Rennie Mackintosh (1868–1928), a Scottish decorator and architect, was one of the leaders of the Art Nouveau movement in Britain. He was a defender of the functionalism in art, and this example of his work typifies his principles that furniture should be slim and taut, based on straight lines and light in colour. It is one of a pair of painted oak cabinets, inlaid with coloured glass, and appeared in 1902.

finish, much of which is the result of polishing by hand with beeswax over hundreds of years.

There are many different methods of surface finishing. The Coromandel technique, for instance, utilized up to a hundred coats of thick lacquer, each applied by hand. When the final coat was hard, the design was then drawn with soft chalk, and the design incised with a sharp blade. The pieces of lacquer were removed and the spaces filled with lacquers of contrasting colours, giving the effect of brightly inlaid metals.

French-polishing

French-polishing started in the 17th century, as a development of the French cabinet-making industry, which used coats of shellac to protect the wood. Up to twelve coats were used creating a skin which, in its crudest form, looked like toffee. When the market demanded something better, an unknown craftsman experimented by adding spirit to the shellac and using linseed oil as a lubricant then rubbing rather than brushing the preparation into the wood. The main tool was a fist-sized pad, known as a "fad". The inside was soaked with oil, and the outside bore the polish itself. This caused the wood to take on a lasting sheen which needed no wax to preserve it. In the 1920s and 1930s French-polishing was used extensively to surface-finish piano cases and high-quality furniture of all kinds, but after World War Two it was superseded by quick-acting spirit-based stains and patent polishes.

Gilding

The gilding, or covering with gold, of wood has a long history. Some pieces of antique French furniture were completely bronze gilded by a tradesman known as a *doreur*, but his secrets have now been totally lost. In the heyday of gilding five methods were used, mercury gilding, matt gilding, gold-leaf gilding—which is still practised—electro gilding and varnish gilding.

Modern finishing

Traditional methods of French-polishing are still in use for fine furniture in craft and other types of workshops, but it is clearly impractical to integrate what can be a lengthy process with the mass production of furniture and other large-scale industrial systems. The growth of mechanized production methods and the application of cost accounting and value analysis—which means getting the best for the least outlay—has meant reorientating wood finishing from a craft to a largely automated system in which chemical engineering has played a large part.

Nitrocellulose

Nitrocellulose lacquer was one of the first of the new finishes, consisting of nitrated cellulose mixed with solvents and plasticizers. Still in use in various forms, it is sprayed on to the wood to form a film. One difficulty with nitrocellulose lacquer is that it softens when it comes into contact with spirits, because it is itself spirit based. A counter-advantage is that a branch of the surface-re-finishing industry specializes in what is known as "pulling over". This means that a spirit film is applied to the deteriorated surface, and a new finish is applied without impairing the appearance. But the basic overall disadvantage is that it remains combustible even when it is dry and hard after years of use. That is the reason why it is not used in locations where there is any fire risk, such as the wood panelling and other furnishings in public transport, including aircraft, and public halls and concert auditoriums.

In industry polymerized mixture is blended in accurate proportions only a short time before use, otherwise catalytic action begins, resulting in a thickening of the mixture which makes it unsuitable for spraying. Another essential factor is the temperature of the spray-shop.

Curtain-coating spreader
Any fluid which pours readily can be applied automatically by this machine, including lacquers, paints, water dispersions, such as colour stains, and a variety of other materials. Another use for the machine is for laying adhesives over flat surfaces in cases where the setting time can be controlled. This makes it particularly useful when door panels are bonded together. The workpieces are moved automatically on feeding belts through a curtain of the fluid. One advantage is that curtain coating will successfully cover bow-shaped, arched and profiled workpieces. In less advanced plants, which use a spray to coat workpieces, there is wastage of the coating, but the curtain coater recycles surplus fluid.

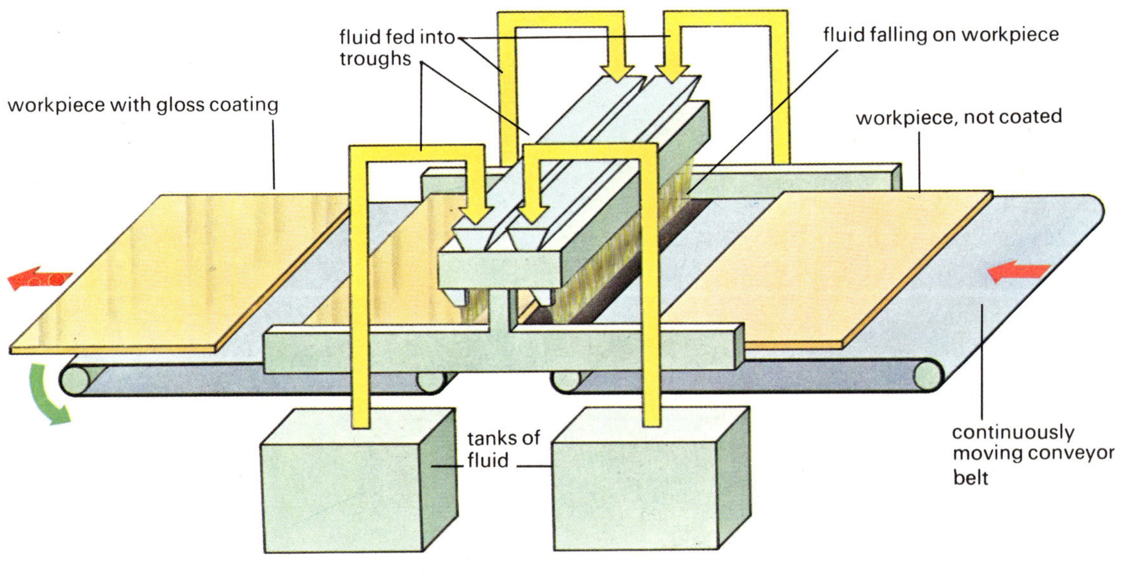

Another innovation is a variation of the "pulling over" method of renovation mentioned earlier. This is done by using pre-mixed finishes containing nitrocellulose so that the finish remains soluble for several days after it has been sprayed on to the wood. After the finish has been "pulled over" to enrobe the surface, polymerization starts and the finish hardens. It is used for special effects in bedroom and other furniture, and when decorative finishes are needed, giving the craftsman time to do his work.

Types of finish

Not all surface finishes have a high sheen. In some cases the buyer may prefer something between a dull matt and a high-gloss sheen. Most of the finishes devised by the laboratories for individual manufacturers can be treated in such a way as to give a matt effect, but this has the disadvantage of weakening the film which covers the wood, giving it a shorter life than the high-gloss finish.

Application of lacquer

In the finishing plant nitrocellulose lacquer and other chemical finishes are sprayed on to the wood. Precision-engineered jets emit the solution in such a way that droplets form in a cloud and fall evenly on to the wood. The rate of spraying combined with the mechanically controlled movement of the wood is critical. If it moves too rapidly, the film will be thin, if it moves slowly it will be thick.

There are other methods of coating the wood. They include the polymer solution being sprayed and reaching the wood by use of an applied electrostatic field of high voltage. In terms of production cost, this system has one major advantage, because it obviates the wastage of polymer. If it does not reach the surface of the wood, it returns to a reservoir and is then recycled.

A less sophisticated method is dipping in which objects like chair legs, entire sections of mass-produced furniture and smaller objects are simply dipped in vats containing finishing solution.

Roller-lacquer spreader
Coatings, from lacquers to paint primers, are applied with this machine, which can operate independently of production lines or incorporated in production processes on a continuous basis. Depending on the material to be applied to the timber, special rubber rollers may be used to ensure even coating, both rollers being driven by an electric motor at a speed of approximately 20m (66ft) per minute, depending on the consistency of the fluid. Because many coatings are relatively expensive, this machine can be adjusted to give a predetermined thickness, and any wastage is caught in a trough and returned to the reservoir.

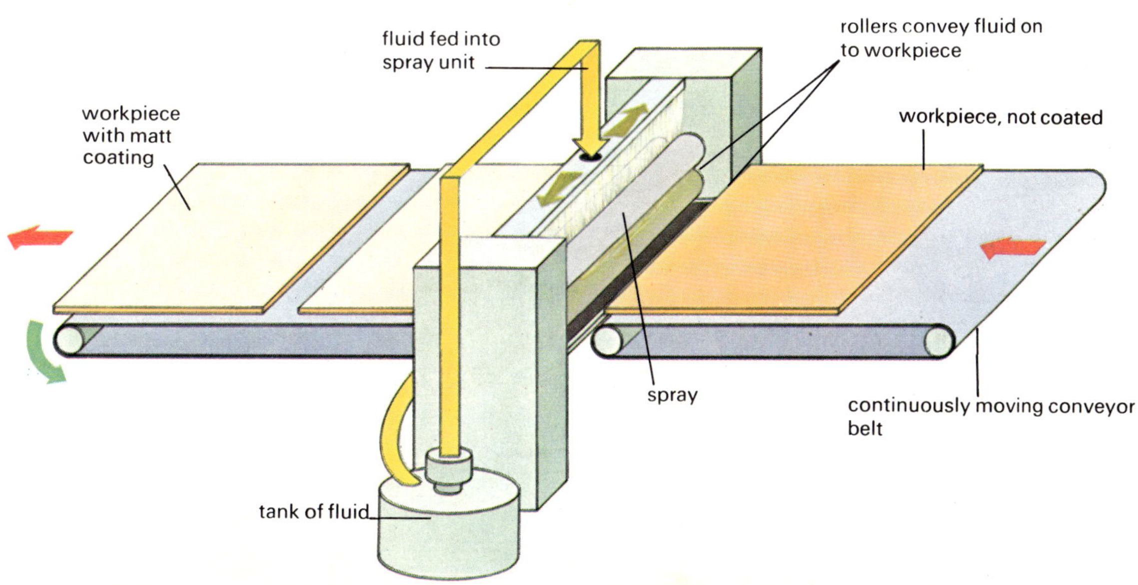

Carving

Ever since trees were first felled wood has been carved. In many cases, wooden or stone figures or decorations are practically all that is left of an entire civilization. In some cases the climate has been kind to the wood and unkind to the stone, which has crumbled. The influence on the development of modern-art trends has been considerable.

▼ String instruments, made in many different countries, are composed of several dozen pieces of carefully selected timber, some for their resonance, others for their stress-bearing qualities. The secret of the fine violin is not only in the timber and construction but also the varnish which preserves the material. Violins are made in different sizes to meet the needs of the child up to the regular concert version. Many antique violins are regarded as art objects in their own right. In 1972 a Stradivari was sold for £21,000.

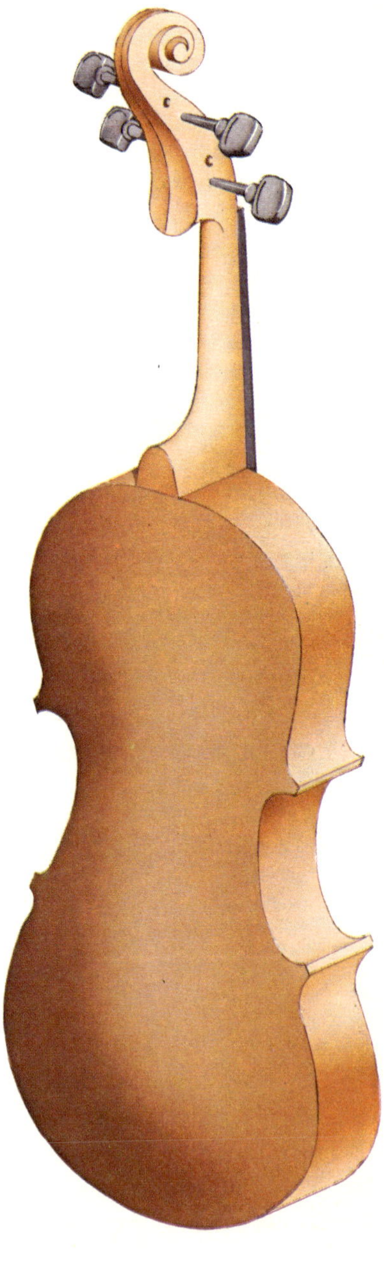

African carving

Most African carvings are unmistakeable in their appearance, and they were made for ceremonial and ritual use. Where cult beliefs were strongest, the carving tended to be the greatest. Probably the best example of this is the work of the Fang tribe, who still live on the Bight of Biafra.

Another African carving genre which has now become well known in Europe and the United States is created by the Makonde, who live on the east coast facing the Indian Ocean. Their work is a form of caricature, with elongated limbs and contorted features. Nowadays, many Makonde carvers work through dealers, imitating the style adopted by their ancestors.

West Africa, with the Ngere, Alangua, Yoruba, Ibo, Ibibio, Fang and Ashira–Bapuna tribes, has always been rich in carvers fashioning masks, figures and wooden figures based on legendary birds and beasts. Even in such areas as Ashanti, where wood carving is relatively rare, and metalwork forms the main basis of expression, carving is still practised and used to decorate ritual stools and thrones, functional head rests and small wooden dolls.

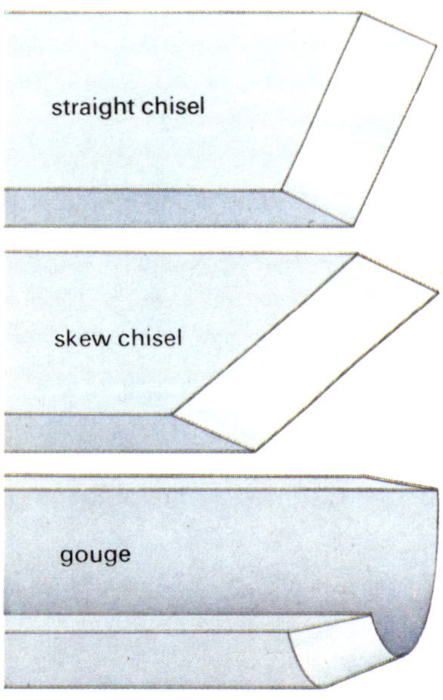

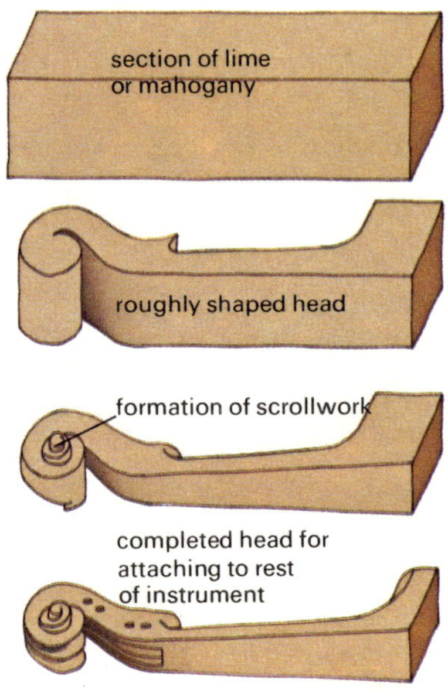

Church carvings

About 1500 years after Christianity was established the story of Christ was told in pictorial form with paintings and wood carvings. They were used to decorate huge cathedrals. Towards the end of the 14th and 15th centuries guilds, or groups of moneyed people, wanted to improve parish churches in their own areas. Carpenters installed hammer-beam roofs, carvers worked on the pews, decorating the ends. Choir stalls were decorated with carved devices not only on the armrests but also the canopies and on the undersides of the tilting seats themselves. Few of these village carvers signed or marked their individual works, and are identifiable only by their style.

Baroque

The pattern of the 17th and 18th century English baroque interior style of decoration was set largely by the wood carver Grinling Gibbons (1648–1721), the most notable of the English woodcarvers. He was commissioned to execute decorative carving for many of the great private houses, public buildings, and churches and cathedrals. Much of his inspiration came from studying still-life paintings of flowers and fruit. His style was to become the densely foliated carving, which is still unsurpassed. He carved out of lime the piece which modern carvers acknowledge to be his finest, the cravat which from a short distance looks like the most delicate lace. It was worn at least once by a monarch, and is nowadays in the Victoria and Albert Museum, London.

English carving tradition was broken by World War Two and the destruction of literally thousands of fine pieces, including a great amount of Grinling Gibbons's best work. Carving continued up to 1939, mainly in the embellishment of furniture, but by 1945 very few master carvers were left in England.

◀ These two Florentine Renaissance heads were created by the London master carver, Gino Masero, to a special commission by private patrons. Such pieces are rarely executed nowadays, due to the lack of patrons willing to let the carver indulge his particular speciality. Masero, with his Italian classical school influences, has restored the work of Grinling Gibbons in many historic buildings, and specializes in the evocation of the golden age of wood carving. Like other master carvers, he does not create pieces for stock, only on commission. In time they will pass into national museums and public collections throughout the world.

Comparison table of timbers

Name	Weight	Shrinkage	Hardness	Workability	Colour
Alder, Red					
Ash					
Ash, Green					
Ash, White					
Basswood					
Beech					
Birch, Grey					
Birch, Yellow					
Cedar, Alaska					
Cedar, Red					
Cedar, White					
Cherry, Black					
Chestnut					
Cypress					
Douglas Fir					
Elder, Box					
Elm					
Eucalyptus					
Fir, Alpine					
Fir, Red					
Fir, White					
Gum, Red					
Hemlock					
Hickory					
Holly					

Shrinkage	Hardness	Workability	Colour
10–20	0% –10%	soft	poor
20–50	10%–20%	medium	fair
50–80	20%–50%	hard	good
80–100	50%–80%	very good	very good

Weight: approx. 0·45kg (1 lb). **Shrinkage:** comparative figures related to a maximum of 200. **Hardness:** comparative figures related to a maximum of 100.

Name	Weight	Shrinkage	Hardness	Workability	Colour
Ironwood					
Larch, Western					
Lignum vitae					
Mahogany W. African					
Mahogany W. Indian					
Maple, Black					
Maple, Red					
Maple, Silver					
Maple, Striped					
Oak, Black					
Pine, Jack					
Pine, Limber					
Pine, Loblolly					
Pine, Norway					
Pine, Pitch					
Pine, White					
Poplar, Yellow					
Redwood					
Spruce, Black					
Spruce, Red					
Spruce, White					
Sycamore					
Walnut					
Willow, Black					
Yew					

Every timber has its main characteristics. This table is a rating of the characteristics, based on the main needs of a variety of trades on the basis that each piece examined is as near perfect as can be.

Table of grain characteristics

Name	Silky	Fine	Close	Straight	Coarse	Inter-locked	Figured	Hard	Soft
Abura		●		●		●		●	
Afara			●	●				●	
Agba		●		●				●	
Alder			●	●				●	
Ash				●	●	●		●	
Beech		●	●	●			●	●	
Birch		●	●	●				●	
Blackbean				●	●			●	
Cedar, European			●	●				●	
Cedar, Canadian	●			●			●		●
Chestnut			●		●	●		●	
Cypress		●		●					●
Ebony			●	●				●	
Elm					●		●	●	
Fir	●	●							●
Gaboon			●	●		●		●	
Greenheart		●		●		●		●	
Guarea		●		●				●	
Gurjun					●	●		●	
Haldu		●		●		●		●	
Hemlock				●			●		●
Hornbeam		●		●				●	
Idigbo	●				●	●		●	
Iroko					●	●	●	●	
Jariah				●	●	●		●	
Larch		●		●					●
Laurel		●		●				●	
Lime	●	●	●	●				●	
Mahogany, African				●	●	●		●	
Mahogany, American				●	●	●	●	●	
Mahogany, S. American	●	●	●				●	●	
Mandio					●			●	
Maple			●					●	

Timber users require comparisons of grain, mainly for interior use, and this is a basic key to what each timber looks like. The user makes a selection and then refers to a book of actual timber specimens to check colour, figuring and other aspects of the selected material.

Name	Silky	Fine	Close	Straight	Coarse	Interlocked	Figured	Hard	Soft
Meranti			■				■	■	
Oak, Europe				■	■		■	■	
Oak, Jap				■				■	
Oak, Silky	■				■			■	
Oak, Tasmanian				■	■		■	■	
Obeche		■		■		■	■		■
Padouk					■	■	■	■	
Pear		■					■	■	
Peroba, Red		■	■	■			■		
Pillarwood		■		■			■		
Pine, Parana		■	■	■					■
Pine, Pitch		■	■	■					■
Pine, White				■	■				■
Pine, Yellow				■					■
Plane		■		■				■	
Podo		■					■		■
Poplar		■		■				■	
Ramin		■		■		■		■	
Rauli	■	■	■	■				■	
Redwood			■						■
Rosewood, S. American			■	■				■	
Rosewood, Indian			■	■	■	■		■	
Sapele				■	■			■	
Satinwood	■	■	■	■		■	■	■	
Spruce, Canadian		■		■					■
Spruce, European	■			■					■
Sycamore	■	■	■	■			■	■	
Teak				■	■		■	■	
Walnut	■			■			■	■	
Walnut, Black American	■			■			■	■	
Willow, European		■		■				■	
Yew		■	■	■			■		■

Make and play Kalaha

In the days of the slave trade in West Africa this game was often played for the winning and losing of slave girls. Although it may at first look very simple, it has many subtleties to it, and the skilled Kalaha player tends to acquire much the same reputation as a Grand Master in chess. It is a game that can be played for fun or with deadly seriousness.

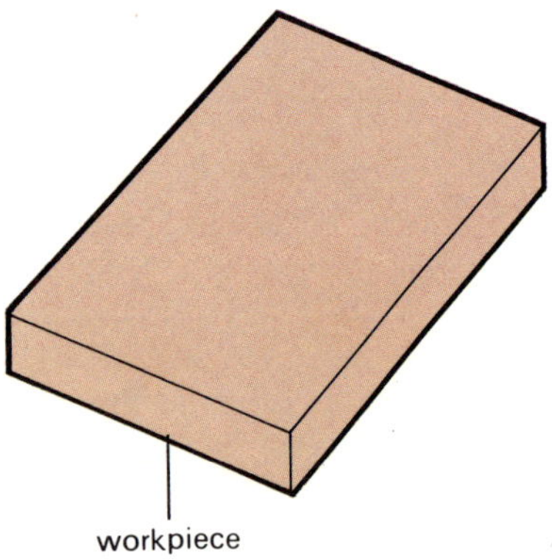

Equipment

The equipment is so elementary that even the beginner in wood-working can make it. A rectangular piece of wood between 30 and 45cm (12 and 18in) long and about 22cm (9in) wide has six cup-shaped hollows on either side, directly opposite each other. If an elaborate Kalaha board is required, rectangular hollows can be made in the centre, one for each of the two players to hold beans that are taken out of the game. These hollows are called *Kalahas*.

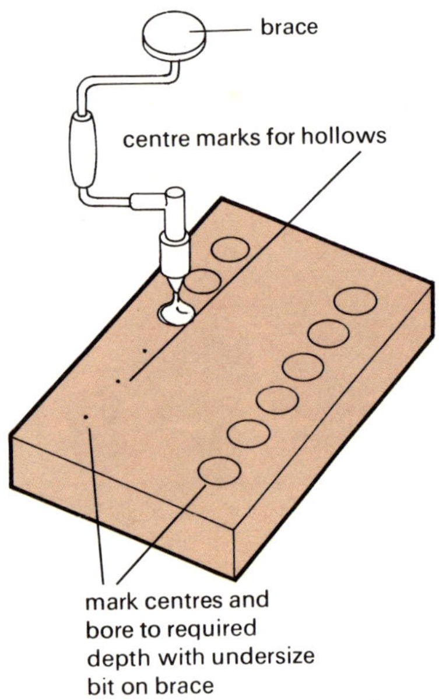

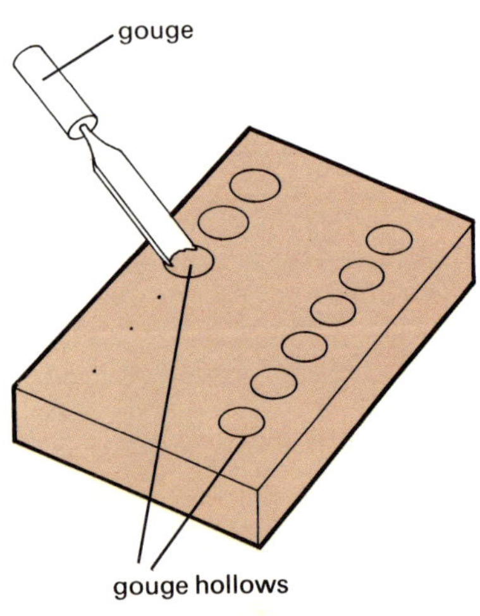

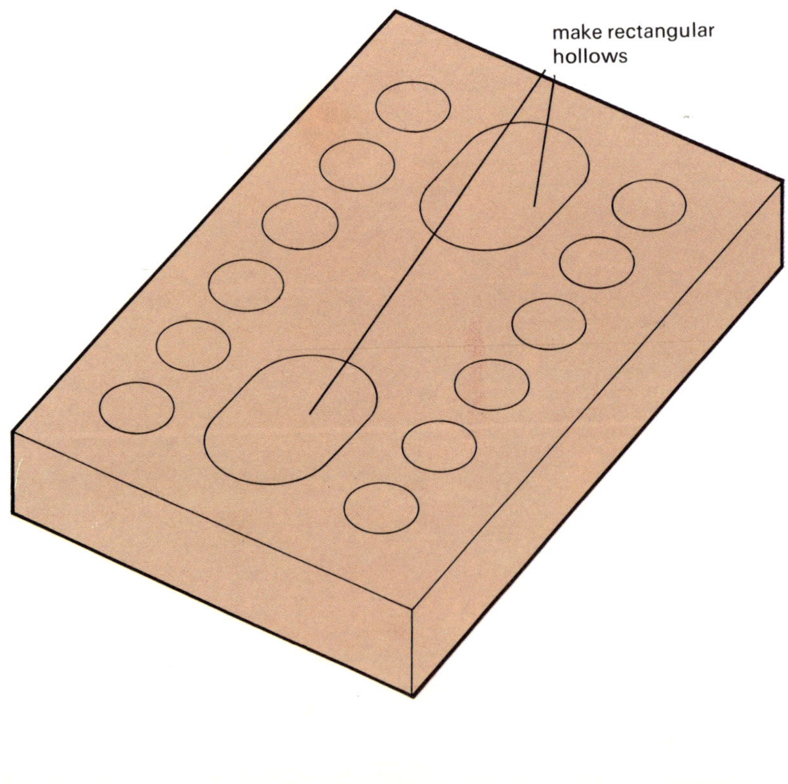

Finishing

The surface finish of the board is entirely the choice of the maker. It can, for instance, be sanded perfectly smooth, and then stained with a spirit or water-based pigment, and, when completely dry, French-polished or given two or three coats of polyurethane, either matt or gloss. A much more elaborate surface decoration can be created by giving it two or three coats of high-gloss white paint, then, when dry, covered with geometric patterns of practically any kind, or Norwegian painted-furniture designs, and finally sealed with polyurethane paint. For the neat surface decorator, the cups themselves could be painted to form faces or cartoon-type features. The most important thing to bear in mind when surface finishing is that the board will get a lot of wear, and so it will have to withstand chipping, which is why a couple of coats of polyurethane paint are recommended.

The 25mm (1 in) diameter cupped hollows can be formed with a brace-and-bit or cut entirely with a carving gouge, which is useful practice for wood carving and sculpture. The only additional equipment needed is three beans for each hollow, making a total of 36 beans.

To play

Each hollow contains three beans. The two players sit one on either side of the board. The purpose of the game is to accumulate as many beans as possible in the Kalaha.

The first player is decided by a throw of dice, top score leading. Each player in turn picks up all the beans from any of the hollows on his side, and throws them, one in each hollow, around the board to the right, including, if there are enough, his own Kalaha, and on into his opponent's hollows (but not his Kalaha). If the player's last ball lands in his own Kalaha, he gets another turn. It can be seen from this that much of the skill of the game is in deciding which hollows to take the beans from.

If the bean lands in an empty hollow on his own side, he captures all his opponent's beans in the opposite hollow and puts them in his own Kalaha together with the capturing bean.

The game is over when all six hollows on one side or another are empty.

All beans in the hollows on the opposite side go into the opponent's Kalaha, and the score is determined by who has the most beans.

The pace of the game is naturally determined by the players. In West Africa it is played very quickly, even by small children, and a single combat may last only a few minutes. In the West, where it has become a calculating, mind-stretching game for executives, or children versus parents, a game may last for up to an hour or even more, because it is possible to play at random and leave the outcome to sheer chance, or by mathematical determination.

A possible game of Kalaha

each hollow contains three beans

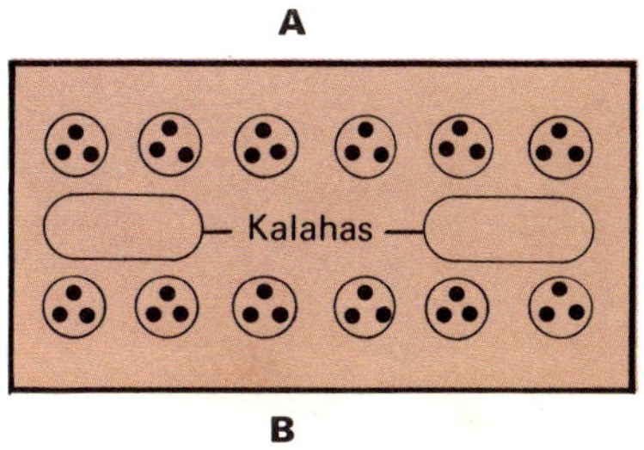

the two players sit on either side of the board

beans removed from this hollow

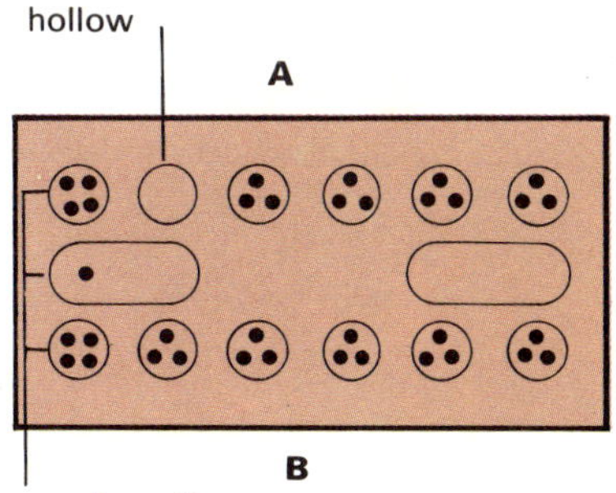

one bean thrown in each hollow to the right
one bean in the Kalaha

a later stage in the game

B has taken eight beans from this hollow and thrown one bean in each hollow moving anti-clockwise

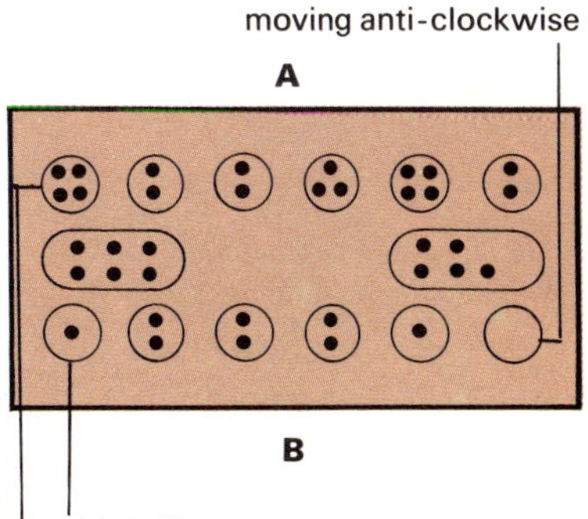

this hollow was empty

B now takes beans from opposite hollow (A's side) and puts them in the Kalaha
B also takes capturing bean

Making wooden jewellery

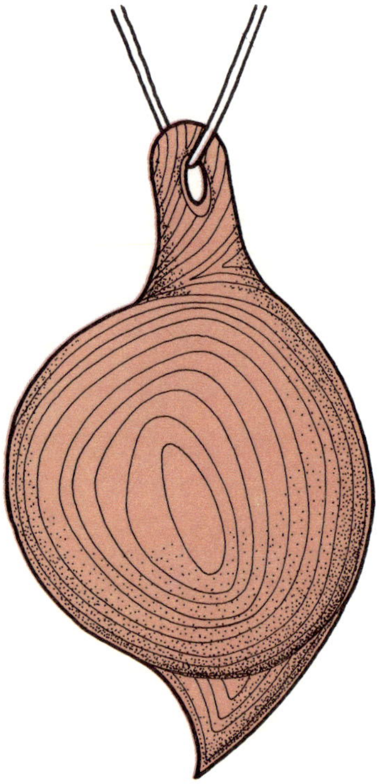

All kinds of things can be done with wood, from cutting it into shapes, and then mounting them on a baseboard, and painting them in a variety of colours, or they can be sanded smooth, stained and wax or French-polished. You can also get parcels of veneer, sold by hobby shops, and create from them a layered effect, then cut through it at an angle with a fretsaw, and build a relief panel suitable for hanging on a wall.

Using plywood

Thick plywood consists of several layers of birch, ash and other timbers, each with its own characteristic colour. Even a small sheet of plywood will yield enough material from which brooches, pendants and badges can be made, using either free-form shapes or strictly geometric ones. If you are using a powered fretsaw or a handsaw, cut the shape at an angle so that all layers can be discerned. Pendants can be finished with the addition of a leather thong or a metal chain, and brooches can have a pin stuck to them with resin-based adhesive. The surface finish can be French-polish or polyurethane matt or gloss paint.

Familiar objects, such as wooden rolling pins, table-tennis bats, stirring spoons and even old wooden bowls, can be sliced up in equal pieces with a powered bandsaw, and then re-assembled in a stepped shape to make decorative objects.

To make attractive raw material for the manufacture of objects, you need only take two or more pieces of different types of timber, making sure that they are all either hardwoods or softwoods, and then use casein glue or one of the waterproof woodworking glues, to stick them all together, one flat plane against another. Leave the piece under pressure or preferably held with cramps for about 24 hours, after which it can be worked into almost any shape you wish, using rasps, saws or power tools.

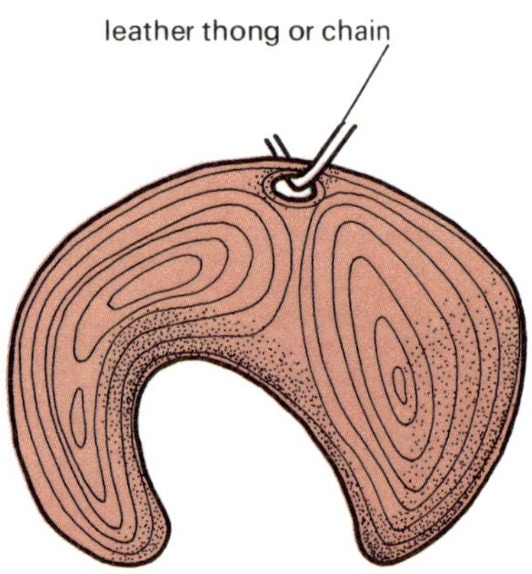

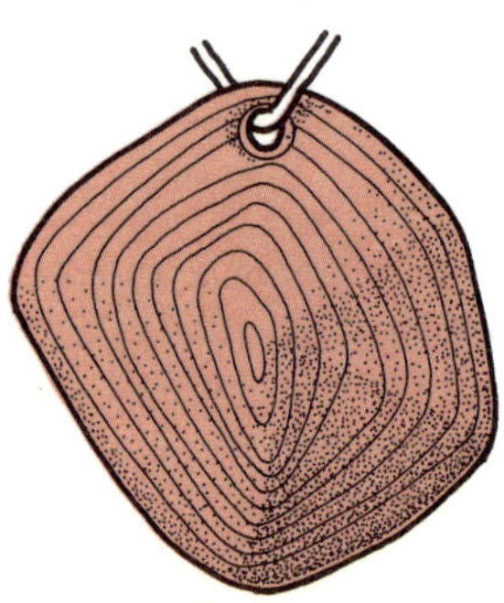

Pendants By letting the imagination roam, practically any shape can be sawn or cut. The only thing to avoid is making a piece so narrow that it will break under the slightest pressure. There is ample scope not only for curvilinear shapes but also bulky and bulbous ones, too.

"Mating surfaces"

If you are really ambitious, you can take odd pieces of wood of all shapes and sizes and create "mating surfaces" by cutting down the angles in such a way as to create as large as possible sections which can be stuck together with one or other of the wood adhesives, clamped and then left to set, usually overnight. These "hybrid" timber sections can be any size you wish, and many amateurs have gone as far as to make occasional pieces of furniture with them, matching the design to the conglomeration of pieces. This sort of mixture of timbers can be power sawn and shaped with the sabre saw or circular saw, and its appearance "in the raw" does not matter very much, because it will be painted and decorated, using brilliant enamels or ordinary household paints. There is one main difference between this sort of furniture and the mass-produced stuff—it will always be unique and it will be a "one off", because the maker will create it in much the same manner as the sculptor works, treating the piece not so much as functional as decorative.

Decoration

Decorating timber of this kind with its mixture of grains and relative hardnesses calls for some ingenuity. Grain, or figuring, is of no consequence, because it will be painted and provided with a "skin" on which the final extravaganza can be laid. Totem poles can be made in the same way, and the individual sections dowelled together, using circular wooden rod which can be bought at any timber shop or yard. The same method can be used to make toys, too. The single essential to keep in mind is that the lines must be bold, there should be an absence of finicky detail. The piece is made and decorated in a deliberately unusual fashion to do one thing, catch the eye of the beholder.

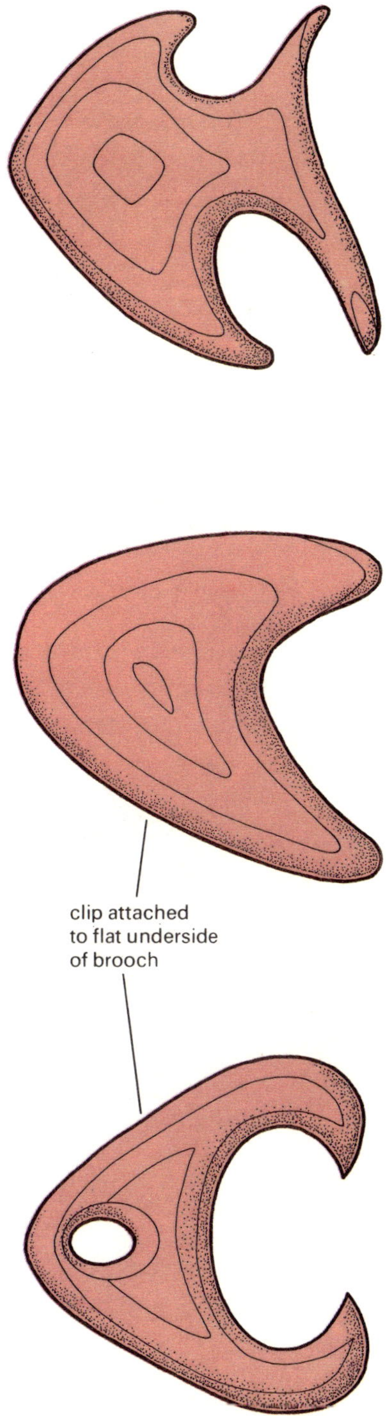

Brooches There is more scope in brooch making, because brooches do not have as much wear as pendants. All these are based on a single tropical fish, but other natural forms can be starting points. The pin fastener, which can be bought from any craft shop, is stuck to the back with a fast-setting resinous adhesive.

Making no-nail furniture

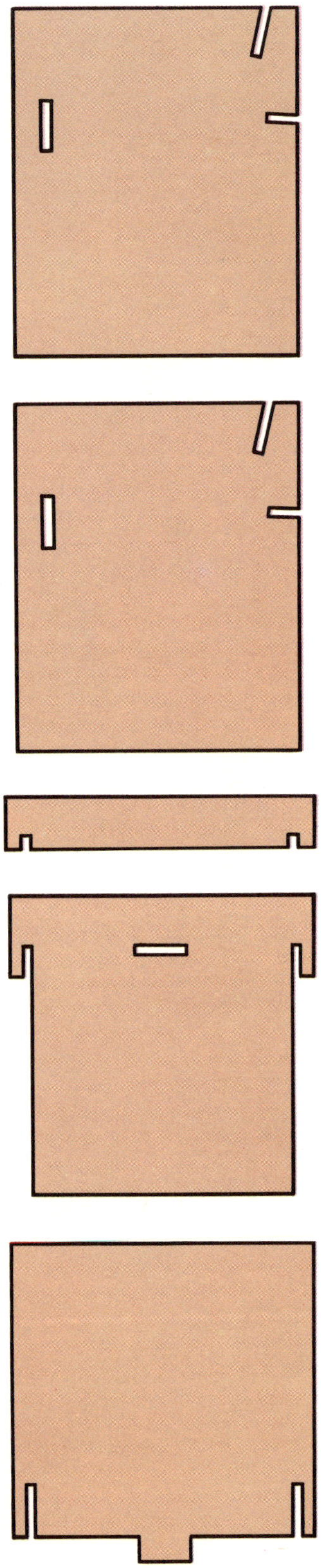

One of the main advantages of making furniture which does not need nails, screws or dowels to hold it together is that it can be pulled apart and moved very easily. It can also be made to fit into practically any space, regardless of size, and yet it will retain its rigidity.

Materials

The basic material is plywood, thickness of which depends on the dimensions of the job and the purpose for which it is to be used. The size 12 is perhaps universally applied for knock-down furniture. It is 12mm ($\frac{1}{2}$in) thick and available in standard-sized sheets 1·5m x 1·5m (60in x 60in) and easily hand sawn, and the edges sandpapered smooth. Depending on the quality, it can be stained and polished, but inferior grades with many knots on one or both sides can be painted a flat or glossy white and then decorated in the traditional Scandinavian fashion.

Slotting chair The lengths of the slots depend on the size of the chair. Theoretically, the chair can be practically any size, from something for the baby up to a construction the size of an armchair. When deciding the size, the thickness, or ply, of the timber should be decided. Obviously, the bigger the chair, the thicker the ply should be, and the length and width of the slots should be sufficiently adequate to provide stability. One other possibility is the curved slot, cut in the style of a piece of jigsaw puzzle, where it is possible to achieve additional tightness and stability.

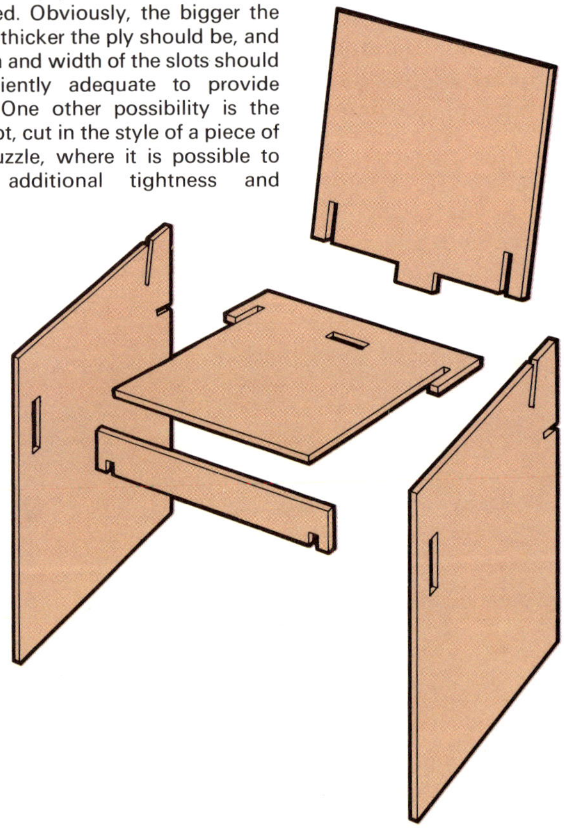

Slot and flange

A first exercise in making nail-less furniture is to build a box, using the slot-and-flange principle shown in the drawing. From this point the box principle is extended so that it becomes possible to vary the dimensions and create furniture like the example in the illustration.

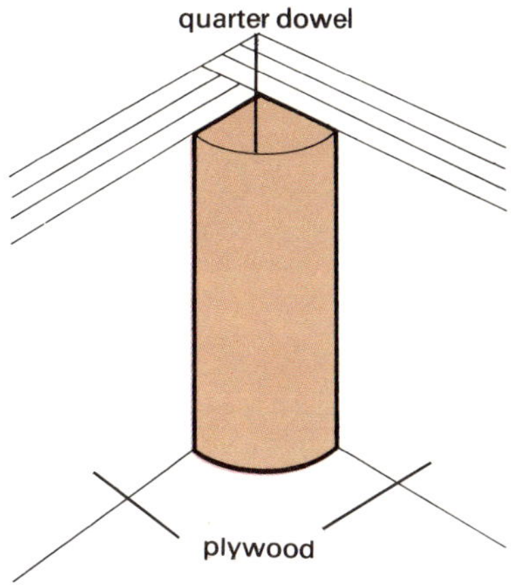

▲ **Dowel fastening** Effective and stable corner fastenings can be made by quarter-sawing a round dowel and then using a generous coating of adhesive on both surfaces. It is generally necessary to apply a corner cramp on the outside for about 24 hours to ensure a lasting joint. The same technique can be used for making plywood boxes and drawers of any size.

Bending plywood

Plywood bends best when it is thin. Thick plywood tends to break or crack when it is under pressure. Birch plywood is the superior plywood for bending, and all that is necessary is a thorough damping with water, after which it can be wrapped round the former, or basic shape, and cramped into position. The formers are simply pieces of scrapwood, which are used in conjunction with cramps to form curves and scrolls. In the case of making wide curves, all that is necessary is to place the sheet of dampened plywood between bricks and leave it overnight.

Another method of making nail-less furniture is to use shop-fitter's catches and the slotted iron strip with nuts and bolts used in industry for making framework for shelving. Hinges can also be used in the inside surfaces of the furniture and stabilized to hold a piece in position.

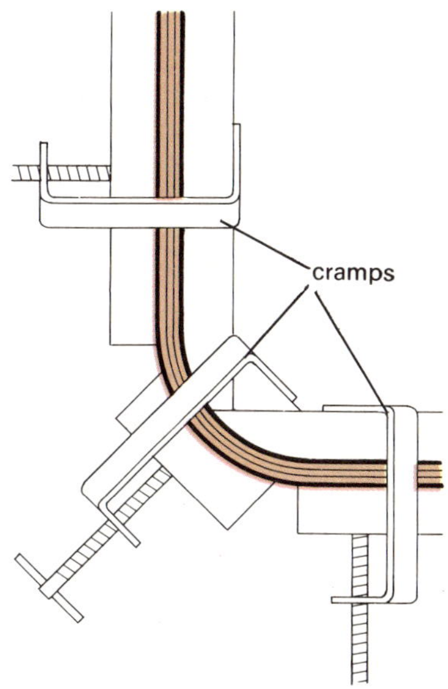

▲ **Cramping** Whenever a cramp is used, its two gripping surfaces must be padded with pieces of plywood to prevent it from damaging the surface of the workpiece. The most common cramp is the G-design, which exerts tremendous pressure, using only hand turning. The pressure should never be increased beyond what is possible with the hand. If greater pressure is needed for a job, then a larger size of cramp should be used.

Dowelling fastening

If fastenings are necessary, they can consist of round dowelling pieces, which are sawn to length to match the length of plywood. A resin adhesive is then applied, and left for about twelve hours, and this should stabilize the corner, or angle. Even large pieces of furniture can be built in this fashion, and a flush fit of the edges ensured. If there are gaps, decorative moulding can be glued along the edge to disguise them. If the piece is to be painted, the moulding can be suitably decorated or gilded.

One of the best ways of working out the method of construction of furniture is to mentally turn the piece inside out so that the problems can be "seen". The golden rule is not to use any external fixings, because they may well look very ugly and unsightly.

Glossary

Adhesives Widely used in timber technology, and dating back to 1793, when animal glues were first applied. Modern synthetic resin adhesives are strong enough to require a force of from 34 to 36 tonnes per centimetre (85 to 90 tons per square inch) before separation or breakage occurs. Other adhesives are casein and starch based.

Bandsaw An electrically-powered continuous saw which uses a flexible blade for cutting contoured shapes.

Bark pockets Occur when the cambium of the growing tree is damaged and bark is drawn into the growth area of the trunk.

Beetles Attack growing or dead timber by boring or general infestation, and include longhorn beetles, pinhole borers, furniture beetles and termites. Other hindrances to growth are the wingless aphids, the miniature spiderlike mites, the stifling larvae of moths and fungal diseases.

Botanical names Every tree has a two-part Latin botanical name, the first indicating the genus, the second the species, for example, *Buxus sempervirens* or European box; *Liquidambar styraciflua* or American red gum; *Pyrus communis* or pear.

Cambium Part of the tree growth, consisting of a delicate tissue between the trunk and the branches. Produces bark by growing outwards and girth enlargement of the trunk by growing inwards.

Cells Timber is composed of brick or tube-shaped cells, some empty, others containing solid or fluid substances. During growth, cells increase in number in the cambium.

Chipboard Internal building material made by cutting many kinds of timber into chips and then reconstituting them in flat boards with a bonding agent.

Circular saw Used as a rule for ripping lengths of timber and powered by an electric motor.

Claw-plate connectors Two plates with metal teeth are used with a nut and bolt to fasten pieces of timber together.

Compression failure Typified by many fine cracks running across the grain. Occurs during growth with the result that seasoned and sawn pieces may later break up and crumble under the slightest pressure. No known reason for the condition.

Conservation In commercial forestry growing areas are carefully planned in such a way as to avoid soil erosion and the unnecessary disturbance of wildlife. Watersheds are defined and assisted to guide moisture to the tree-growing areas.

Dichotomous key Term used to classify a timber by bringing together a given number of features, such as moisture content, the presence of oils and resins, the speed with which moisture can be removed, and oils and resins measures. The key is used partly to decide the use to which any batch of timber may be put and whether it is suitable for external or internal use.

Differential shrinkage The process which occurs when timber is seasoned. Every timber behaves differently during seasoning, and a knowledge of internal structural changes by experts can determine the use to which a particular batch is put.

Deformation Part of laboratory testing to discover the extent to which a timber sample will return to its original shape after being subjected to a series of forces, such as compression and bending.

Elasticity Part of the laboratory measurement of a sample piece of timber to discover what will happen after it reaches the final phase before it breaks.

Fibre saturation point The situation in which all water has been drawn out of the timber, leaving the cell walls saturated to a percentage of between 25 and 30 per cent of the dry weight of the cells.

Figuring Term used to describe the patterns caused by the arrangement of tissues in timber.

Forces In construction work of any size a variety of forces are at work in the interplay between timber beams, ceiling and floor and floor joists and supports. Architects and builders use research-laboratory reports to determine the limits to which they can go when building houses and other constructions.

Fuel Timber is used by many world areas as a fuel. About 2300 million tonnes (2300 million tons) are burned annually for domestic or industrial purposes.

Growth rings Concentric layers of tissue in the tree, each is created by the cambium during the growing season. The rings are layers of wood, one is added each year.

Gum veins Dark streaks found in certain timbers and, typically, in hardwoods.

Hardwoods One of two commercial classifications of timber, the other being softwoods. Hardwoods are dicotyledons, which are broad-leaved and with seeds in seed-cases.

Heartwood Section of trunk in the centre, providing rigidity and a support for the crown, or top, of the tree.

Housing Buildings have been made of timber for thousands of years. The latest versions used stressed-skin plywood construction techniques. Timber housing is common in such countries as New Zealand, Australia, Germany, Canada and America.

Knots They are created while the tree is growing and form at points where branches meet the trunk. They can be a serious problem in construction work if they appear at strategic points, weakening the timber.

Latex canals They may cause splits in some timbers, such as the tropical jelutong and mujua. Microscopically, they are either tubular or cellular. Timber with many canals may still be used as the core of some constructions or, in some cases, for decorative purposes.

Leaves They collect nourishment from air by photosynthesis, which occurs as a result of sunlight causing the leaf vessels containing chlorophyll to react. By a chain reaction, this leads to the making of essential sugars and starches. Most leaves live up to six months and are then replaced by new growth.

Maximum load The point in laboratory testing of a timber sample at which the fibres break and part.

Mineral streaks Seen as dark or light streaks, and not regarded as a serious defect if the timber is being used for construction purposes.

Moisture One of the most important factors in considering the use to which any particular timber can be put. Water exerts a strong influence over the behaviour of timber. To determine the amount in a sample, the piece is first weighed and then dried for a specific period in a special oven, and then re-weighed to discover how much water has been drawn off.

Nitrocellulose Material used as the basis of surface finishing of furniture.

Paper Made in part from spruce with the addition of recycled waste paper, rags, grass and other materials.

Permanent set The point in laboratory testing at which a timber sample breaks when it is bent.

Pith flecks Caused by the tunnelling of insect larvae, it represents a defect in timber intended for commercial use, but sometimes an asset in veneers and pieces used for decorative purposes.

Planing machine A powered machine, generally with a continuous drum-shaped blade for the production of smoothed sections, including battens and door panels.

Plywood Made by building up layers of two or more wood veneers. The plies run in opposing directions, imparting strength and flexibility.

Resin Found in softwoods. It forms in cells and in some species may form canals or ducts running vertical to the stem growth. Common in most of the pines and spruce.

Roots The tree growth in the earth, spreading in radial and other directions. They take water from the soil, and mineral salts and oxygen to help nourish the growth.

Router Part of wood machining equipment, consisting of a powerful, fast-running motor and interchangeable cutting heads to shape pieces of timber.

Sapwood Varies in various trees from a narrow to a broad band, consisting of new growth. The purpose is to conduct the nutritious sap and store food.

Seasoning Used to describe the drying out of surplus moisture and conditioning of new timber. Commercially, seasoning utilizes forced-draught humidity-controlled kilns. In primitive conditions timber is air-seasoned by stacking under barn-type roofs and allowing the air to circulate freely.

Shakes A term used in the timber trade to describe splits caused by the opening of the grain.

Shear plates Flush-fitting connectors used to fasten pieces of timber together.

Softwoods One of two commercial classifications of timber, the other being hardwoods. Softwoods are gymosperms or conifers, which are cone-bearing with needle-shaped leaves and naked seeds.

Stress testing A laboratory process to determine changes in the shape of a timber sample.

Split-ring connectors Simple metal fittings used to fasten together two pieces of timber.

Strawberry marks They are round red-coloured areas found in some spruce, and caused by resin accumulation.

Specific strength The ratio of strength to any given unit weight, used by designers, architects and builders when considering the use of timber in specific situations and locations.

Toughness Each type of timber has its own point at which it will break. This and its reaction to the impact of nails, dowels, screws and fastening devices is classified as toughness. The term is relative to the job which has to be done by the timber.

Turning One of the most ancient woodworking crafts, using a foot-powered treadle or electric lathe. Modern turning lathes operate at 400 to 2000 rpm. The purpose is to make round sections for use as chair and table legs, columns and even large pillars.

Veneer Thinly-sliced or peeled timber, generally tropical in origin, used to face the body of furniture and decorative objects, or for the manufacture of plywood.

Bibliography

H. E. Desch, *Timber: Its Structure and Properties* (Macmillan, 1968). A comprehensive textbook on timber keyed to the Institute of Wood Science third-year syllabus, and containing a wealth of scientific observation.

E. R. Huggard, *Foresters' Engineering Handbook* (Heffer, 1958). A description of civil-engineering methods in forestry operation.

Hugh Johnson, *International Book of Trees* (Mitchell Beazley, 1973). Covers the life cycles of more than 600 trees, and gives some hints on how to plant and grow trees.

Jack H. Leigh, *The Timber Trade: An Introduction to Commercial Aspects* (Pergamon, 1971). Useful for the study of how the timber trade operates, including helpful notes on the business in many different countries.

Alan Mitchell, *A Field Guide to the Trees of Britain and Northern Europe* (Collins, 1974). A systematic guide to tree species with many measurements and scientific data about habitat.

Frederick Oughton, *The Finishing and Refining of Wood* (Constable, 1969). How the wood finisher works to produce beauty from the bare wood, enhancing work of the cabinet maker and creator of fine furniture.

Frederick Oughton, *The History and Practice of Wood Carving* (Allman, 1969). A standard work on woodcarving with many historical notes and instructions on how to carve wood.

Frederick Oughton, *Woodworking Tools* (Constable, 1973). The history of tools that originated in Egypt, Italy, Russia, Sicily and Germany, and have not undergone any marked changes.

Index